LABOR LAW

Second Edition

by
Margaret C. Jasper

Oceana's Legal Almanac Series:
Law for the Layperson

2002
Oceana Publications, Inc.
Dobbs Ferry, New York

#50137063

Library of Congress Control Number: 2002101869

ISBN: 0-379-11365-1

Oceana's Legal Almanac Series: Law for the Layperson
ISSN 1075-7376

Manufactured in the United States of America on acid-free paper.

To My Husband Chris

Your love and support
are my motivation and inspiration

-and-

In memory of my son, Jimmy

Table of Contents

CHAPTER 3:
THE NATIONAL LABOR RELATIONS BOARD

CHAPTER 4:
OBTAINING UNION REPRESENTATION

CHAPTER 5:
COLLECTIVE BARGAINING

CHAPTER 6:
UNFAIR LABOR PRACTICES

CHAPTER 7:
CONCERTED ACTIVITY

CHAPTER 8:
THE FEDERAL LABOR RELATIONS AUTHORITY

APPENDICES

ABOUT THE AUTHOR

MARGARET C. JASPER is an attorney engaged in the general practice of law in South Salem, New York, concentrating in the areas of personal injury and entertainment law. Ms. Jasper holds a Juris Doctor degree from Pace University School of Law, White Plains, New York, is a member of the New York and Connecticut bars, and is certified to practice before the United States District Courts for the Southern and Eastern Districts of New York, the United States Court of Appeals for the Second Circuit, and the United States Supreme Court.

Ms. Jasper has been appointed to the panel of arbitrators of the American Arbitration Association and the law guardian panel for the Family Court of the State of New York, is a member of the Association of Trial Lawyers of America, and is a New York State licensed real estate broker and member of the Westchester County Board of Realtors, operating as Jasper Real Estate, in South Salem, New York. Margaret Jasper maintains a website at http://members.aol.com/JasperLaw.

Ms. Jasper is the author and general editor of the following legal almanacs: Juvenile Justice and Children's Law; Marriage and Divorce; Estate Planning; The Law of Contracts; The Law of Dispute Resolution; Law for the Small Business Owner; The Law of Personal Injury; Real Estate Law for the Homeowner and Broker; Everyday Legal Forms; Dictionary of Selected Legal Terms; The Law of Medical Malpractice; The Law of Product Liability; The Law of No-Fault Insurance; The Law of Immigration; The Law of Libel and Slander; The Law of Buying and Selling; Elder Law; The Right to Die; AIDS Law; The Law of Obscenity and Pornography; The Law of Child Custody; The Law of Debt Collection; Consumer Rights Law; Bankruptcy Law for the Individual Debtor; Victim's Rights Law; Animal Rights Law; Workers' Compensation Law; Employee Rights in the Workplace; Probate Law; Environmental Law; Labor Law; The Americans with Disabilities Act; The Law of Capital Punishment; Education Law; The Law of Violence Against Women; Landlord-Tenant Law; Insurance Law; Religion and the Law; Commercial Law; Motor Vehicle Law; Social Security Law; The Law of Drunk Driving; The Law of Speech and the First Amendment; Employment Discrimination Under Title VII; Hospital Liability Law; Home Mortgage Law Primer; Copyright Law; Patent Law; Trademark Law; Special Education Law; The Law of Attachment and Garnishment; Banks and their Customers; and Credit Cards and the Law.

INTRODUCTION

This almanac presents an overview of the area of law known as labor law. The common-law and legislative history of labor relations in the United States is explored, including the evolution of the National Labor Relations Act, as amended and interpreted by the applicable case law.

Labor law encompasses all aspects of labor/management relations including the rights of workers to organize and form unions; the process of collective bargaining; the obligations the law places on employers and unions in the collective bargaining process; prohibitions against unfair labor practices; and the role of the National Labor Relations Board in enforcing the process.

This almanac also discusses the role of the Federal Labor Relations Authority (FLRA) in resolving labor/management disputes in the Federal sector and enforcing compliance with the Civil Service Reform Act of 1978.

The Appendix provides the text of applicable statutes and other pertinent information and data. The Glossary contains definitions of many of the terms used throughout the almanac.

There are many other legal issues concerning the employer/employee relationship which may be of particular interest to the reader, including matters relating to discrimination, harassment, fair pay, health and safety, and pension and retirement benefits. A discussion of those areas of employment law may be found in this author's almanac entitled Employee Rights in the Workplace, also published by Oceana Publishing Company.

CHAPTER 1:
HISTORICAL DEVELOPMENT OF
LABOR LAW

ENGLISH COMMON LAW

In England, Parliament refrained from legislating in areas involving workers and employers due to the prevailing policy of laissez-faire. The earliest
law affecting labor was passed in 1802 and dealt with the health, safety,
and morals of children employed in textile mills. Subsequent laws dealt
with hours and conditions of employment.

Labor unions were legalized in 1825, however, agreements to seek better
hours and wages were punishable as common law conspiracy until 1871
and 1906, when such agreements were finally legalized.

COLONIAL LAW

In colonial America, forced labor systems such as slavery and indentured
servitude were legal, however, regulations were nonetheless passed limit-
ing a master's control over his servants and slaves. As in England, labor
organizing in the United States was discouraged by the common law doctrine that unions represented a conspiracy against the public good.

EARLY NINETEENTH CENTURY

In the 19th century, labor laws were passed which were designed to improve working conditions. Slavery ended with the Civil War and indentured servitude disappeared by 1910. Although Federal employees were
granted a 10-hour workday in 1840, the Supreme court did not recognize
the legality of state laws that limited the workday to 8 hours until 1908.

Nevertheless, unionizing was still considered criminal conduct, and workers who engaged in concerted activities, such as picketing and striking,
were subject to prosecution for criminal conspiracy. Courts generally
granted prosecutors wide authority to indict union leaders for violence or
property damage that occurred during a strike. This harsh common-law

rule led to a public outcry, and in the mid-nineteenth century, the criminal sanctions gave way to civil liability.

During this time period, the Courts were concerned with protecting employers, and routinely issued injunctions to prevent strikes. Employers sought and were awarded monetary damages. Under the prima facie tort doctrine, Courts held that intentional infliction of economic harm was tortious conduct unless there was some underlying legitimate purpose. These civil cases were decided by judges who had a wide variety of opinions on union activity and the purposes that would be deemed legitimate. This led to quite unpredictable and conflicting opinions among the courts.

The Industrial Revolution introduced factory production and greatly expanded the class of workers dependent on wages as their source of income. The terms of the labor contract, including working conditions and the relationship between workers and employers became an utmost concern to the public.

EARLY TWENTIETH CENTURY

As the unions continued to push for recognition into the early 20th century, their activities were further confined by the Federal judiciary. The Federal Courts used the Sherman Antitrust Act to punish any union activity that had the effect of restraining trade. Most union organizing involves tactics that necessarily restrain trade, e.g. strikes and boycotts.

Through the first three decades of the 20th century, employers enjoyed a pro-management era that was successful in thwarting most union activity. Injunctions were readily available, and quite effective in suppressing union activity.

WORLD WAR I

By the time World War I began in 1917, the American labor movement had grown to three million workers. In 1918, in order to promote peace between labor and management, President Woodrow Wilson created the War Labor Board. The War Labor Board recognized the "right of workers to organize in trade unions and to bargain collectively through chosen representatives." The War Labor Board was a mediation tool which did not have any enforcement power. The War Labor Board handled approximately 1,200 cases affecting 700,000 workers. Through its efforts, labor and management agreed to refrain from strikes or lockouts during this time of war.

POST-WORLD WAR I

Once the war ended in 1918, this former peaceful relationship between labor and management also came to a close. Unions lost major strikes and union membership dropped drastically. Labor-management relations were particularly hostile during this period. Pro-labor sentiment resulted in the issuance of injunctions to stop strikes.

In 1926, the Railway Labor Act was passed, which recognized the importance of collective bargaining to minimize strikes and lockouts on railways. The Railway Labor Act gave railroad workers the right to select their own bargaining representatives "without interference, influence or coercion."

THE GREAT DEPRESSION

As a result of the Great Depression of the 1930's, Congress sought ways to promote peace among the American workforce in order to improve the national economy. In 1932, Congress passed the Norris-LaGuardia Act, which checked the power of the courts to issue injunctions or restraining orders against strikes, where there was no violence or fraud involved. Congress also declared that workers had the right to bargain collectively and unionize.

THE NEW DEAL

As part of President Franklin Roosevelt's New Deal policies, the government committed itself to cooperate with industry. In this connection, the National Industrial Recovery Act ("NIRA") was passed in 1933. This Act allowed employers within a single industry to form trade associations that set production quotas or fixed prices under "Codes of Fair Competition" (the "NIRA Codes).

In return, employers stipulated that these Codes would establish minimum wages, maximum hours, and other conditions of employment. The Act also guaranteed workers the right to bargain collectively and join unions of their choice without coercion or interference from employers. The Act also provided that employers would not require their workers to join company unions. Nevertheless, the Act did not contain any enforcement provisions. Following passage of this Act, there was a renewed interest in unionizing, however, many employers reneged and refused to recognize certain unions.

NATIONAL LABOR BOARD

Because employers failed to comply with the labor policy set forth in the Act, there was much unrest among workers and an increase in strikes. This led to the creation of the National Labor Board to temporarily enforce the provisions of the Act. The President appointed Senator Robert Wagner of New York as Board Chairman and formalized the Board's power with an Executive Order which authorized the Board to conduct union representation elections and handle violations of the NIRA Codes.

The NLB had some minimal success in settling labor disputes, however, because its enforcement powers were limited, it was not very successful in achieving voluntary compliance with the Act. Thus, in 1934, Senator Wagner introduced a bill seeking to establish a permanent agency to mediate labor disputes which would have greater enforcement powers. In 1934, Congress compromised and authorized the President to establish the National Labor Relations Board. Nevertheless this early version of the present NLRB also lacked the enforcement power necessary to enforce Section 7(a) of the NIRA.

During the mid-1930's, the labor movement continued to grow rapidly. Strikes were being conducted regularly and the economy failed to improve. In 1935, the U.S. Supreme Court ruled that the National Industrial Recovery Act was unconstitutional.

THE NATIONAL LABOR RELATIONS ACT

In 1935, Senator Wagner introduced the National Labor Relations Act ("NLRA")—also referred to as "The Wagner Act"—which sought to create a new independent agency to enforce rights rather than merely mediate disputes. The NLRA would require employers to bargain collectively with unions selected by a majority of employees in an appropriate bargaining unit. The NLRA covered most workers in industries which affected interstate commerce. The NLRA was passed in 1935.

The constitutionality of the NLRA rested on the argument that employers' interference with the right of workers to unionize and refusal to bargain collectively negatively interfered with interstate commerce. Opponents to the law unsuccessfully challenged this argument when in 1937, the U.S. Supreme Court upheld its constitutionality in a 5-4 decision.

The NLRA created a permanent board of three members and gave it broad enforcement tools, including subpoena power and the right to issue cease-and-desist orders enforceable in court. It also gave the Board the power to order remedies for violations, including employee reinstatement, back pay, and good faith bargaining. The law also forbid employers from restraining, interfering with or coercing employees in the exercise of their rights to unionize and bargain collectively through representatives of their own choosing. Under the original Act, unfair labor practices were only assessed against employers.

An overview of the National Labor Relations Act is set forth in Chapter 2 and specific provisions of the NLRA are explored in detail in this almanac.

WORLD WAR II

In December 1941, after America entered World War II, concerned that labor disputes could disrupt production of war machinery, President Roosevelt created the National War Labor Board. The Board had the power to mediate and arbitrate disputes. A labor-management conference was held at which the parties agreed to reciprocal no-strike/no-lockout provisions so that the nation's industrial strength would not be undermined by labor unrest.

POST-WORLD WAR II

The end of World War II saw an increase in strike activity by unions which felt that they had lost ground as a result of the strict wartime controls. However, the post-war public expressed a strong anti-strike sentiment and began to view organized labor as becoming too powerful. As a result, revisions to the pro-labor Wagner Act were proposed.

In particular, the original Act only addressed unfair labor practices by employers. Senator Taft introduced legislation which proposed to make unions subject to unfair labor practices under the Act. Congressman Hartley also proposed a bill that was more restrictive on labor. A compromise was reached and the Labor-Management Relations Act—also referred to as "The Taft-Hartley Act"—was passed.

The Labor-Management Relations Act is discussed more fully in Chapter 2.

THE MCCLELLAN COMMITTEE

In the mid-1950's, organized labor came under intense scrutiny by Congress for corruption and racketeering. This led to a number of hearings by the Senate Select Committee on Improper Activities in the Labor Management Field—also referred to as "The McClellan Committee." Congress found that some unions, among other things, had accepted bribes from management, misappropriated union funds and failed to maintain proper records.

As a result, in 1959, Congress enacted the Labor-Management Reporting and Disclosure Act—also referred to as "The Landrum-Griffin Act." This Act protected employees' union membership rights from unfair practices by unions, while the NLRA protected employee rights from unfair practices by employers or unions.

PRESENT DAY

In the 1980's, it appeared that the pro-labor movement started to lose ground again. Laws and court decisions limited labor and the power of labor unions. Cutbacks in federal agencies reduced federal enforcement of many work safety rules. The Reagan and Bush administrations attempted to reduce labor regulations, arguing that they made U.S. industry less competitive in the world market.

In 1990, the Supreme Court ruled against two management tactics that were routinely used during the 1980's. The Court made it harder for companies to replace union workers with nonunion workers and also restricted the ability of a company to use bankruptcy laws to avoid paying pensions,

By the late 1990s, overall union membership had increased, however, the number of union members in the private sector and the percentage of union workers compared to nonunion workers had decreased.

CHAPTER 2:
FEDERAL LEGISLATION

THE RAILWAY LABOR ACT

The Railway Labor Act (RLA), enacted in 1926, is the first statute governing labor relations to be passed in the United States. The RLA applies to labor relations on railroads, and was amended in 1936 to include jurisdiction over interstate airlines. The RLA does not cover labor relations in the private sector.

THE NORRIS-LAGUARDIA ACT

It was not until the passage of the Norris-LaGuardia Act in 1932 that things began to change for labor relations within the private sector. A significant change was the removal of the Federal Court's authority to issue injunctions in nonviolent labor disputes. Lawful union conduct recognized by the statute could no longer be enjoined by the Federal Courts.

THE NATIONAL LABOR RELATIONS ACT

In 1935, the National Labor Relations Act (the "NLRA") was passed. The NLRA—also known as The Wagner Act—is the primary body of Federal Law governing labor-management relations in the private sector. Excluded from coverage under the NLRA is employment subject to the Railway Labor Act, employment in the federal sector, and employment by states or their political subdivisions.

The NLRA's goal was to equalize the playing field by supporting unionization. The Act championed union rights by prohibiting conduct by employers which infringed upon those rights and implementing the national labor policy of assuring free choice and encouraging collective bargaining as a means of maintaining industrial peace. The original Act did not contain any provisions which prohibited union conduct and was thus viewed as a pro-employee/anti-employer statute.

The NLRA also established the National Labor Relations Board (the "NLRB" or "Board), which is the administrative agency responsible for carrying out the provisions of the Act. The purpose, function and structure of the NLRB is discussed further in Chapter 3 of this almanac.

Through the years, Congress has amended the Act, and the National Labor Relations Board, as well as the judicial system, have developed a body of law drawn from the statute. As discussed further in this almanac, the most significant sections of The Act include the following:

Section 7

Section 7 of the NLRA guarantees the right of employees to organize and to bargain collectively with their employers or to refrain from all such activity, and provides that:

> Employees shall have the right to self-organization, to form, join or assist labor organizations to bargain collectively through representatives of their own choosing, and to engage in other concerted activities for the purpose of collective bargaining or other mutual aid or protection, and shall also have the right to refrain from any or all of such activities except to the extent that such right may be affected by an agreement requiring membership in a labor organization as a condition of employment as authorized in Section 8(a)(3).

Section 7 affords employees greater bargaining power. Once a union is engaged in bargaining, individual employees cannot break out and bargain on their own. However, Section 7 does allow employees to take certain action, such as strikes or picketing.

Examples of employee rights protected by Section 7 include:

1. The right to form or attempt to form a union among the employees of a company.

2. The right to join a union whether the union is recognized by the employer or not.

3. The right to assist a union in organizing the employees of an employer.

4. The right to go out on strike to secure better working conditions.

5. The right to refrain from activity on behalf of a union.

Section 8

Section 8 of the Act lists conduct deemed to be an unfair labor practice under the Act. It is through Section 8 that the rights afforded by Section 7 are enforced. Section 8 sets forth illegal employer acts known as unfair labor practices ("ULPs"), and authorizes the governing agency to order an employer to cease and desist such practices. Section 8 basically prohibits:

1. Employer interference with an employee's Section 7 rights (§8(a)(1));

2. The formation of company unions (§8(a)(2));

3. Employers from taking discriminatory action against employees due to union activity (§8(a)(3));

4. Employers from taking discriminatory action against employees who testify or bring charges before the governing agency (§8(a)(4)); and

Section 8 also requires employers to bargain collectively with the recognized representative of the employees (§8(a)(5)).

Section 9

In Section 9 of the NLRA, the procedures for choosing a particular bargaining representative—i.e., a union—are set forth.

The text of the National Labor Relations Act is set forth at Appendix 1.

THE LABOR MANAGEMENT RELATIONS ACT

During the depression, union activity increased amid a growing anti-labor sentiment. The NLRA provided no restrictions on union activity. There was concern that the unions were abusing their new-found power and the Board was viewed as anti-employer. This led to the 1947 enactment of the Labor Management Relations Act (the "LMRA")—also known as the Taft-Hartley Act. The LMRA endeavored to neutralize the playing field between labor and management.

The LMRA amended Section 8 of the NLRA, adding Section 8(b) which, for the first time, set forth prohibited union activities, such as secondary boycotts. In addition, Section 7 of the NLRA was amended to give employees the right to "refrain" from unionizing. The LMRA also made closed shops illegal and gave the President the power to secure an injunction to postpone for 80 days any strike that might affect the national security. In addition, under the Act, officers of unions were required to file affidavits that they were not members of the Communist party.

The Act also gave the Court of Appeals greater review authority of Board decisions. It guaranteed employers "free speech," however, employers were still prohibited from making threats or engaging in reprisals.

Under the Act, unions were also made chargeable with unfair labor practices in violation of Section 8. For example, employees have the right to get rid of a union with which they are dissatisfied. This is known as a "decertification" procedure. If the union makes threats against the employees, this is chargeable as an unfair labor practice.

In addition, the Act established the Office of the General Counsel to the Board, which took over prosecuting unfair labor practices, a function that the Board previously handled.

The text of the Labor Management Relations Act is set forth at Appendix 2.

THE LABOR/MANAGEMENT REPORTING AND DISCLOSURE ACT

The Labor/Management Reporting and Disclosure Act (the "LMRDA")—also known as the Landrum-Griffin Act—was passed in 1959 in response to reported financial abuses of union funds by union officers. The LMRDA established a "bill of rights" for union members which gives the members the right to financial disclosure, the right to sue their own union, and civil and criminal remedies against union officers guilty of financial abuse. The Act also confers union members the right to participate in union elections in the capacity of both candidate and voter.

The LMRDA also amended the Taft-Hartley Act in a number of respects. Among other things, state courts and state labor relations boards were given jurisdiction over cases declined by the Board under its jurisdictional standards, and prohibitions against secondary boycotts were tightened. In addition, a new unfair labor practice made it unlawful for a union to picket for recognition or organizational purposes in certain circumstances.

CHAPTER 3:
THE NATIONAL LABOR RELATIONS BOARD

IN GENERAL

The National Labor Relations Board (the "NLRB" or "Board") is an independent federal agency created by Congress in 1935 to administer the National Labor Relations Act. As set forth in Chapter 2, the NLRA is the primary law governing labor relations between unions and employers in the private sector who engage in business affecting interstate commerce. The statute guarantees the right of employees to organize and to bargain collectively with their employers or to refrain from all such activity. However, the Act does not govern airlines, railroads, agriculture, and government agencies.

The Board's basic purpose is to formulate a national labor policy to promote industrial peace and facilitate interstate commerce. In particular, the Board is responsible for administering the representation provisions of the Act, and determining unfair labor practices. The Board also regulates the conduct of elections. Through the years, Congress has amended the Act and the Board and courts have developed a body of law drawn from the statute.

Selected provisions of the NLRB Rules and Regulations are set forth at Appendix 3.

BOARD FUNCTIONS

The Board has two principal functions:

1. To determine, through secret-ballot elections, whether employees wish to be represented by a union in dealing with their employers and, if so, by which union; and

2. To prevent and remedy unlawful acts, called unfair labor practices, committed by employers or unions.

The Board does not act on its own motion in either function. It processes only those petitions for employee elections and unfair labor practice charges that are filed with one of its 52 regional, subregional, or resident offices.

A directory of NLRB regional and subregional offices is set forth at Appendix 4 and a directory of resident offices is set forth at Appendix 5.

The Board is further empowered by the Act:

1. To conduct secret-ballot elections among employees who are represented by a union to determine whether or not they wish to revoke their union's authority—a process known as "decertification"—upon request by at least 30 percent of the employees;

2. To determine in cases involving jurisdictional disputes which of the competing groups of workers is to be assigned the work task involved; and

3. To conduct secret-ballot elections among employees in national emergency situations.

The Board exercises full and final authority over the Office of the Executive Secretary and the Office of the Solicitor. It appoints administrative law judges and, subject to the provisions of the Administrative Procedure Act and Section 4(a) of the National Labor Relations Act, exercises authority over the Division of Judges.

Each Board Member exercises full and final authority over a staff of legal counsel who are under the immediate supervision of the chief counsel of the respective Board Member. The Board, with the General Counsel, approves the budget, opens new offices as deemed necessary, and appoints Regional Directors and officers in charge. The Board also establishes and publishes the Agency's Rules and Regulations and Statements of Procedure.

NLRB STRUCTURE

Board Members

The Board, composed of five Members, has its central and principal office in Washington, D.C. Each Board Member is appointed by the President, with the approval of the Senate, for a term of 5 years. One Member is designated by the President to serve as Chairman of the Board. The Board primarily acts as a quasi-judicial body in deciding cases on the basis of formal records in administrative proceedings.

There is a great deal of political influence placed on the Board, and whether a Board is "Republican" or "Democrat" has been known to influence its decisions. For example, the "Eisenhower Board" agitated labor whereas the "Kennedy Board" was known to agitate management.

The current members of the Board are Peter J. Hurtgen (Chairman), Wilma B. Liebman, Michael J. Bartlett, and William B. Cowen. One seat is vacant.

A directory of the Board and its staff members is set forth at Appendix 6.

Office of the Executive Secretary

The Office of the Executive Secretary, as the chief administrative and judicial management officer of the Board, represents the Board in dealing with parties to cases. The Office: (i) communicates on behalf of the Board with labor organizations, employers, employees, members of Congress, other agencies, and the public; (ii) receives, dockets, and acknowledges all formal documents filed with the Board; (iii) issues and serves on the parties to cases all Board Decisions and Orders; and (iv) certifies copies of all documents which are a part of the Board's files or records.

Office of the Solicitor

The Solicitor is the Board's chief legal officer and advises the Board on: (i) questions of law and policy; (ii) adoption, revision, or rescission of Rules and Regulations and Statements of Procedure; (iii) pending legislation amending or affecting the Act; and (iv) litigation affecting the Board, etc.

The Office of the Solicitor also drafts advisory opinions and declaratory orders for the Board concerning whether the Board would assert jurisdiction in a particular case.

The Division of Judges

The Division of Judges is comprised of administrative law judges who are responsible for conducting hearings and preparing decisions in unfair labor practice cases. The Chief Administrative Law Judge supervises the operation of the Division of Judges and has final authority to: (i) designate the administrative law judges who will conduct hearings and make rulings; (ii) assign dates for hearings presided over by administrative law judges; and (iii) rule upon requests for extensions of time within which to file briefs, proposed findings, and conclusions.

The Division of Information

The Division of Information coordinates the Board's information and public relations programs by conducting briefings and disseminating information of Board activities through the news media and to companies, unions, law firms, academic groups, and others. The Information Office also arranges for distribution of decisions and summaries of decisions to interested parties.

The Office of the General Counsel

The General Counsel is independent from the Board and is responsible for the investigation and prosecution of unfair labor practice cases and for the general supervision of the Board field offices in the processing of cases. The current General Counsel is Arthur F. Rosenfeld

The General Counsel is appointed by the President, with the approval of the Senate, for a term of 4 years. The General Counsel derives specific authority for some functions of the office from the provisions of section 3(d) of the National Labor Relations Act, and derives certain other authority by delegation from the Board.

The General Counsel exercises general supervision over attorneys employed by the Board, and over the officers and employees in the Regional Offices. The General Counsel does not have authority over administrative law judges, legal counsel to Board members, the Executive Secretary, or the Solicitor.

The General Counsel has final authority, on behalf of the Board, to: (i) investigate charges and issue complaints under section 10 of the Act; (ii) prosecute such complaints before the Board; (iii) prosecute injunction proceedings pursuant to section 10(e) and 10(j) of the Act; (iv) handle Court of Appeals proceedings to enforce or review Board orders; (v) perform other miscellaneous court litigation; (vi) obtain compliance with Board orders; (vii) oversee the processing of representation petitions by field personnel under section 9 of the Act; and (viii) handle jurisdictional disputes under section 10(k) of the Act.

The Deputy General Counsel is vested with the authority to speak and act for the General Counsel in all phases of the responsibilities of the office to the full extent permitted by law, and is responsible for overall coordination of the General Counsel's organization.

The General Counsel's Washington Staff

The General Counsel's Washington staff, reporting to the General Counsel and the Deputy General Counsel, is comprised of four main divisions: (i) The Division of Operations Management; (ii) The Division of Advice; (iii) The Division of Enforcement Litigation; and (iv) The Division of Administration.

The Division of Operations Management.

The Division of Operations Management is headed by the Associate General Counsel for Operations Management, whose responsibilities include: (i) assisting in the coordination and integration of all operations in Washington with the field offices; (ii) developing systematic methods for the integration of case processing activities in all field and Washington operational units; (iii) implementing General Counsel and Board policies, including time and quality standards for case processing at all stages; (iv) continuing liaison with field offices; and (v) supervising and coordinating both substantive and administrative phases of the operations.

The Division of Advice

The Division of Advice is headed by the Associate General Counsel for Advice, whose responsibilities include: (i) researching labor law administration; (ii) providing legal advice to Regional Directors on all unfair labor practice cases involving novel or difficult legal issues, including questions involving mandatory or discretionary injunction proceedings; (iii) litigating injunction cases on appeal from a district court; (iv) maintaining legal information retrieval systems; and (v) compiling digests to be used by both the Board staff and the public.

The Division of Enforcement Litigation

The Division of Enforcement Litigation is headed by the Associate General Counsel for Enforcement Litigation, whose responsibilities include all Board litigation in the United States Courts of Appeals and the Supreme Court of the United States, whether within the General Counsel's statutory authorization or delegated by the Board, including contempt litigation and enforcement and review of Decisions and Orders of the Board. It is also responsible for miscellaneous litigation in Federal and state courts to protect the Board's procedures and functions.

The Office of Appeals

The Office of Appeals is a principal part of the Division of Enforcement Litigation. This office reviews appeals from Regional Directors' refusals to issue complaints in unfair labor practice cases and recommends the action to be taken by the General Counsel. Pursuant to request, the Director of the Office of Appeals may also hear informal oral argument by counsel or other representatives of the parties in support of, or in opposition to, the appeals.

The Division of Administration

The Division of Administration is headed by the Director of Administration whose responsibilities include: (i) administrative management; (ii) support services; and (iii) fiscal functions of the General Counsel. These activities are carried out with the assistance of branches dealing with financial management, personnel, facilities and services, data systems, management and audit, security and safety, and library services. These functions, as applicable, are also performed on behalf of the Board and its Members.

Regional Offices

There are 33 Regional Offices through which the Board conducts its business. Some of the Regions have Subregional Offices or Resident Offices in addition to the central Regional Office.

Each Regional Office is headed by a Regional Director appointed by the Board on the recommendation of the General Counsel and includes: (i) a Regional Attorney: (ii) an Assistant to the Regional Director; (iii) field attorneys; (iv) field examiners; and (v) clerical staff. Each Subregional Office is headed by an officer in charge appointed in the same manner as the Regional Directors. Each Resident Office is headed by a Resident Officer. The responsibilities and functions of these positions are discussed below.

Regional Directors

Under the general supervision of the Office of the General Counsel, the Regional Directors supervise a staff of attorneys and field examiners in the processing of representation, unfair labor practice, and jurisdictional dispute cases. The Regional Director is responsible for making the initial determination in cases arising within the geographical area served by the region.

The Regional Directors are empowered to: (i) issue notices of hearing in representation cases; (ii) issue complaints in unfair labor practice cases; (iii) conduct elections pursuant to agreement of the parties, or to direct elections in the absence of such agreement; (iv) issue certification of representatives or certify the results of elections where appropriate; (v) obtain settlement of unfair labor practice charges; (vi) obtain compliance with administrative law judge, Board, and court decisions; (vii) investigate, report on, and decide objections to elections and challenges to determinative ballots; and (viii) otherwise act on behalf of the General Counsel in the discharge of the statutory and delegated functions of that office.

In addition, Regional Directors may initiate and prosecute injunctions pursuant to Section 10(1) of the Act in the District Courts. They also have authority to process petitions for unit clarification, for amendment of certification, and for rescission of a labor organization's authority to make an agreement pursuant to section 8(a)(3).

Regional Attorneys.

The Regional Attorneys are the principal legal advisors to the Regional Directors and, as the chief legal officers in the Regions, exercise supervisory authority over office attorneys and field examiners in various aspects of their work. They may exercise any authority given attorneys and field examiners in the Regions.

Assistants to the Regional Directors

The responsibilities of the Assistants to the Regional Directors include: (i) overall supervision and coordination of investigations and compliance; (ii) exercising supervisory authority over office attorneys and field examiners in various aspects of their work; (iii) providing assistance to the Regional Director with respect to various administrative functions.

Field Attorneys

The Field Attorneys are charged in general with the duty of performing all necessary legal services for the Regional Directors in the Regions. They are directly responsible to the Regional Attorneys, and through them to the Regional Directors, for performance of these services.

Under the direction of the Regional Attorneys, Field Attorneys: (i) investigate petitions concerning the representation of employees—including the taking of secret ballots of employees—in accordance with section 9(c) of the National Labor Relations Act; (ii) conduct hearings in proceedings under section 9 of the National Labor Relations Act and section 7(b) of the Fair Labor Standards Act; (iii) investigate charges of unfair labor practices under section 8 of the Act; (iv) appear and participate as counsel in Board hearings and, when designated, in other Board litigation and proceedings; (v) prosecute any inquiry necessary to the functions of the General Counsel; and (vi) perform all necessary acts required of them in connection with the foregoing and the published Rules and Regulations of the Board.

In connection with these duties, Field Attorneys have the right to access and copy evidence, administer oaths and affirmations, examine witnesses, and receive evidence.

Field Examiners

The Field Examiners are directly responsible to the Regional Directors and work under their direction. Their responsibilities include: (i) investigating petitions concerning the representation of employees in accordance with section 9 of the Act; (ii) conducting secret-ballot elections where such procedure is required under the Act; (iii) investigating charges of unfair labor practices under section 8 of the Act; (iv) conducting hearings in proceedings under section 9 of the Act and section 7(d) of the Fair Labor Standards Act; (v) performing all necessary acts in connection with the foregoing and the published Rules and Regulations of the Board.

Field Representatives also have the right to access and copy evidence, administer oaths and affirmations, examine witnesses, and receive evidence.

Officers in Charge and Resident Officers

The Officer in Charge of a Subregional Office and the Resident Officer of a Resident Office are directly responsible to the Regional Director and, under his direction, supervise the processing of cases arising within the geographical area of the office. Under special delegation from the General Counsel, an Officer in Charge may be authorized to exercise the functions of the Regional Director, subject to statutory limitations.

JURISDICTION

By federal statute, the Board has exclusive jurisdiction over industries that affect interstate commerce. Nevertheless, the Board has limited its own jurisdiction. The Board took the position that it would better serve the purposes of the Act if it limited its jurisdiction to industries whose operations have a substantial impact on the flow of interstate commerce. The Board determines its jurisdictional standards by analyzing both the type of industry and the amount of annual business realized by the particular industry.

The Board's standards in effect as of July 1, 1990, are as follows:

1. *Nonretail Business*: Direct sales of goods to consumers in other States, or indirect sales through others, of at least $50,000 a year; or direct purchases of goods from suppliers in other States, or indirect purchases through others, of at least $50,000 a year.

2. *Office Buildings*: Total annual revenue of $100,000 of which $25,000 or more is derived from organizations that meet any of the standards except the indirect outflow and indirect inflow standards established for nonretail enterprises.

3. *Retail Enterprises*: At least $500,000 total annual volume of business.

4. *Public Utilities*: At least $250,000 total annual volume of business, or $50,000 direct or indirect outflow or inflow.

5. *Newspapers*: At least $200,000 total annual volume of business.

6. *Radio, Telegraph, Television, and Telephone Enterprises*: At least $100,000 total annual volume of business.

7. *Hotels, Motels, and Residential Apartment Houses*: At least $500,000 total annual volume of business.

8. *Privately Operated Health Care Institutions*: At least $250,000 total annual volume of business for hospitals; at least $100,000 for nursing homes, visiting nurses associations, and related facilities; at least $250,000 for all other types of private health care institutions defined in the 1974 amendments to the Act as "any hospital, convalescent hospital, health maintenance organizations, health clinic, nursing home, extended care facility or other institution devoted to the care of the sick, infirm, or aged person." Public hospitals are excluded from NLRB jurisdiction by Section 2(2) of the Act.

9. *Transportation Enterprise, Links and Channels of Interstate Commerce*: At least $50,000 total annual income from furnishing interstate passenger and freight transportation services; also performing services valued at $50,000 or more for businesses which meet any of the jurisdictional standards except the indirect outflow and indirect inflow of standards established for nonretail enterprises.

10. *Transit Systems*: At least $250,000 total annual volume of business.

11. *Taxicab Companies*: At least $500,000 total annual volume of business.

12. *Associations*: These are regarded as a single employer in that the annual business of all association members is totaled to determine whether any of the standards apply.

13. *Enterprises in the Territories and the District of Columbia*: The jurisdictional standards apply in the Territories; and all businesses in the District of Columbia come under NLRB jurisdiction.

14. *National Defense*: Jurisdiction is asserted over all enterprises affecting commerce when their operations have a substantial impact on national defense, whether the enterprises satisfy any other standard.

15. *Private Universities and Colleges*: At least $1 million gross annual revenue from all sources (excluding contributions not available for operating expenses because of limitations imposed by the grantor).

16. *Symphony Orchestras*: At least $1 million gross annual revenue from all sources (excluding contributions not available for operating expenses because of limitations imposed by the grantor).

17. *Law Firms and Legal Assistance Programs*: At least $250,000 gross annual revenues.

18. *Employers that Provide Social Services*: At least $250,000 gross annual revenues.

19. *Gambling Casinos*: The Board also asserts jurisdiction over gambling casinos when these enterprises are legally operated, and when their total annual revenue from gambling is at least $500,000.

In addition to the above, through enactment of the 1970 Postal Reorganization Act, jurisdiction of the NLRB was extended to the United States Postal Service, effective July 1, 1971.

Ordinarily, if an enterprise does the total annual volume of business listed in the standard, it will necessarily be engaged in activities that "affect" commerce. The Board must find, however, based on evidence, that the enterprise does in fact "affect" commerce. However, the Board has established the policy that when an employer whose operations "affect" commerce refuses to supply the Board with information concerning total annual business, the Board may dispense with this requirement and exercise jurisdiction.

Finally, Section 14(c)(1) authorizes the Board, in its discretion, to decline to exercise jurisdiction over any class or category of employers when a labor dispute involving such employees is not sufficiently substantial to warrant the exercise of jurisdiction, provided that it cannot refuse to exercise jurisdiction over any labor dispute over which it would have asserted jurisdiction under the standards it had in effect on August 1, 1959. In accordance with this provision the Board has determined that it will not exercise jurisdiction over racetracks, owners, breeders, and trainers of racehorses, and real estate brokers.

The Act also excludes certain individuals from its jurisdiction, including:

1. Agricultural laborers.

2. Domestic servants.

3. Any individual employed by his parent or spouse.

4. Independent contractors.

5. Supervisors.

6. Individuals employed by an employer subject to the Railway Labor Act.

7. Government employees, including those employed by the U .S. Government, any Government corporation or Federal Reserve Bank, or

any State or political subdivision such as a city, town, or school district.

8. Supervisory and managerial employees are also excluded from the protection of the Act.

In addition, the Act excludes certain employers from its jurisdiction, including:

1. The United States or any State Government, or any political subdivision of either, or any Government corporation or Federal Reserve Bank.

2. Any employer subject to the Railway Labor Act.

For entities not subject to the NLRA, information concerning the labor law of a particular state may be obtained by contacting that state's Department of Labor.

A Directory of State Departments of Labor is set forth at Appendix 7.

PUBLIC INFORMATION PROGRAM

Information concerning the National Labor Relations Board may be obtained by contacting the NLRB's Information Officer in any one of the 52 field offices. The Information Office helps the public prepare unfair labor practice charges and representation petitions and provides referrals to other federal or local agencies, if appropriate. If a charge or petition is sought, the Information Officer generally completes the filing process the same day.

Conversations With America

Conversations with America is a government initiative designed to engage federal workers in "conversations" with the public. These conversations take place in many settings and for the purpose of providing information and discussing ways to improve government services. The National Labor Relations Board and its Regional offices regularly sponsor seminars and conferences that focus on developments in the National Labor Relations Act and other labor and employment laws, and discussions of NLRB regulations, policies and practices. NLRB representatives, including Board Members, General Counsel and Regional Directors, are available to answer questions and discuss concerns. Regional Offices also hold Open Houses that provide customers with an opportunity to discuss their opinions and concerns. For information on the scheduling of these events, the reader is advised to contact their local NLRB Regional Office.

Additional information may be obtained by contacting NLRB Headquarters:

THE NATIONAL LABOR RELATIONS BOARD
Franklin Court Building, Suite 5530
1099 14th Street, NW
Washington, DC 20570-0001
Telephone: (202) 208-3000

CHAPTER 4:
OBTAINING UNION REPRESENTATION

IN GENERAL

If a group of employees wishes to unionize, the process is generally initiated by asking a union for representation. While the employees are discussing unionization, their employer is prohibited from interfering with such discussions.

If the employer is disruptive or otherwise tries to end union discussions, the employees can file a violation with the Board even though they don't yet belong to a union. Employees cannot be fired for attempting to exercise their Section 7 right to organize, even in jurisdictions which subscribe to the employment at will doctrine.

PETITION FOR REPRESENTATION ELECTION

The Board is responsible for determining whether the employees should be represented by a particular union. To initiate the process, a petition for a representation election is filed with the Board. This is known as a "representation case."

A sample NLRB Representation Petition is set forth at Appendix 8.

A representation case is usually filed by a labor union, although a petition for representation may be filed by an employee; a group of employees; or an employer. The petition is filed with the Board's regional office.

In seeking representation, the petitioner must show that 30 percent of the employees in a particular bargaining unit desire unionization. This is usually accomplished by the filing of authorization cards with the petition. Authorization cards are signed and dated by the employee, and demonstrate the employee's support for the particular union. The cards are kept secret from the employer so that it cannot determine which employees are union sympathizers.

When a representation petition is filed, the Board sends all parties to the case a copy of the petition. Most petitions seek to have the Board conduct a secret-ballot representation election. The Board will explore any issues which are necessary to resolve before an election can be conducted. The Regional Director investigates to make sure there are no bars to an election, and that the Board has proper jurisdiction over the employer.

The Board may ask the parties to submit their legal arguments. Some petitions may be dismissed. Once it is determined that there are no impediments to an election, the possibility of holding a consent election is explored. A consent election requires the agreement of both the union and employer. According to NLRB statistics, the Board has been successful in achieving election agreements 80 percent of the time.

REPRESENTATION HEARING

If the Regional Director is unable to get the parties to agree to a consent election, a representation hearing will be ordered, at which all interested parties appear and argue their respective positions concerning the propriety of an election. The appropriate bargaining unit is identified and a determination is made as to which employees will be able to vote in an election.

Based upon the evidence, the Regional Director decides whether an election should be held. A written decision will be issued promptly. The time it takes to issue a decision may depend upon the length of the hearing, complexity of issues and office work load.

According to the NLRB, from the time a petition is first filed, a regional decision after hearing should normally issue within 45 days. A party may request review of the Regional Director's decision by the Board in Washington, DC. From the time a regional decision after hearing issues, the parties should expect that an election normally will be conducted, if appropriate, within 25 to 30 days.

THE ELECTION

Where an election is deemed appropriate, the Board will conduct a secret-ballot election in such a manner so as to provide the eligible employees in the appropriate collective-bargaining unit an opportunity to cast their ballot. The Board attempts to schedule the election as soon as practicable, normally within 6 to 8 weeks after the petition has been filed.

The election is normally held either at the place of employment or at the regional office. Votes are cast by secret ballot. Although an employee is not required to vote in the election, they are nonetheless bound by the majority vote. The union is bound to fairly represent all of the employees in the particular bargaining unit.

Following the election, the losing party may file objections to the results if there is an allegation that the winner was guilty of misconduct, or if there was some other problem involving the election. The Regional Director decides whether the objections have any merit, and issues a decision as to whether the election results will be set aside or validated.

CERTIFICATION AND EXCLUSIVITY

Following the resolution of any challenged ballots or objections, the Board will certify that a union is the collective-bargaining representative of the employees in the voting unit.

Section 9 of the NLRA provides that representatives designated or selected for the purposes of collective bargaining by the majority of the employees in a unit appropriate for such purposes, shall be the exclusive representatives of all the employees in such unit for the purposes of collective bargaining.

Exclusivity is the cornerstone of the National Labor Relations Act. Once certified, a union is the exclusive bargaining agent for a certified unit. A union is deemed "certified" when the Board designates it as the bargaining representative after a valid representation election has been held.

The Certification Bar

The union's exclusive authority cannot be challenged for at least one year. This is known as the 1-year certification bar, which runs from the date of certification. During this period:

1. No decertification petitions are allowed;

2. No rival union petitions are allowed; and

3. The employer must bargain with the certified union.

To avoid the 1-year certification bar, a union and employer can agree to "recognize" the union without going through a Board election.

Decertification

A decertification petition may be filed with the Board by an employee, a group of employees, or a union on their behalf, pursuant to Section 9(e)(1) of the NLRA. As with a certification petition, a decertification petition must be accompanied by a showing that at least 30 percent of the employees in the bargaining unit support decertification of the existing union.

The Board will review the petition and order a secret ballot election. Although an employer is not permitted to file a decertification petition, it may refuse to bargain with the existing union while the petition is pending.

APPEALABILITY OF BOARD REPRESENTATION PROCEDURES

Under Section 10(f) of the NLRA, aggrieved persons are permitted to petition the Court of Appeals for review of a final order. For example, judicial review is available for decisions in unfair labor practice cases because such decisions are considered final orders.

However, decisions approving or denying union certification are not considered final orders. Therefore, a union which is denied certification has no appellate relief. Nevertheless, an employer may be able to obtain appellate review of such a decision in a more roundabout manner.

For example, if the employer objects to certification of a particular union on representational grounds, e.g., union misconduct, it may thereafter refuse to bargain with the union. The employer's refusal to bargain may generate a Section 8(a)(5) charge by the union that the employer is engaging in an unfair labor practice for refusing to bargain.

Once the Board issues an order requiring the employer to bargain, the employer's continued refusal will force the case to the Court of Appeals for enforcement. At this point, the employer can raise the representation issues as its defense, thereby obtaining judicial review.

IDENTIFYING THE APPROPRIATE BARGAINING UNIT

The bargaining unit must be defined in the petition. The bargaining unit must be appropriate, i.e., the members must have common interests. A unit of employees is a group of two or more employees who share a community of interest and may reasonably be grouped together for purposes of collective bargaining. The determination of what is an appropriate unit for such purposes is, under Section 9(b) of the Act, left to the discretion of the NLRB.

To determine the appropriateness of a bargaining unit, the Board looks to see whether the proposed unit shares a "community of interests"—i.e., whether there is similarity in benefits, wages, type of work, skills, and qualifications, etc.

In addition, the Board may also consider the following factors:

1. The bargaining history of the employee;

2. The bargaining history of the industry;

3. Any conflict of units among workers; and

4. The physical proximity of the employees.

Prior Board determinations and past bargaining history cannot be the sole basis for a decision.

Professional vs. Non-Professional Unit

Professionals have a federally protected statutory right not to be included in a unit which contains non-professionals. Section 9(b)(1) of the Act provides that:

> The Board shall decide in each case the unit appropriate for the purposes of collective bargaining provided, that the Board shall not decide that any unit is appropriate for such purposes if such unit includes both professional employees and employees who are not professional employees, unless a majority of such professional employees vote for inclusion in such unit.

The professionals' statutory right was challenged in *Leedom v. Kyne* (1958), wherein a professional engineers' association (the "Association") petitioned the Board for certification as the exclusive bargaining agent for all 233 nonsupervisory professional employees of a Westinghouse plant. A rival union wanted to represent both the 233 professionals and 9 non-professionals.

A Board hearing was held and the Board determined that the 9 non-professionals should be included in the bargaining unit due to their close interests with the professional employees. The Association asked for a vote to see if the majority of professionals wanted the non-professionals included in the unit.

The Board refused to take the vote and ordered an election to see who would be the exclusive bargaining representative of the entire unit. The Association moved for a stay of the election pending exclusion of the non-professionals from the bargaining unit. The Board denied the motion. The Association won the election and was certified as the unit's bargaining representative.

Following the election, the Association brought suit in Federal District Court against the Board requesting that the Board's actions be set aside and the 9 non-professionals be excluded from the bargaining unit. The trial court found that the Board violated Section 9(b)(1) in that it denied the professionals their federally protected statutory right.

The Board appealed the ruling arguing that the Federal Court does not have jurisdiction to tamper with Board orders in a certification proceeding because they are not final orders and thus not appealable, unless they involve unfair labor practices.

However, both the Court of Appeals and the U.S. Supreme Court affirmed the trial court's ruling on appeal, holding that Federal Courts do have jurisdiction over Board orders in certification proceedings in the limited situation where a Federal statute is thereby violated.

Multi-Employer Bargaining Units

Multi-employer bargaining involves bargaining between a union and a group of employers. Although the employers remain separate, they reach a common agreement with the union that applies to all of the employers who are parties to the agreement.

Multi-employer bargaining may confer benefits on both the union and the employers who are parties to the agreement. For example, it controls competition between employers insofar as it establishes common benefits, wages and working conditions. In addition, it permits the union to negotiate less but cover more employees.

To create a Board-certified multi-employer bargaining unit, there must be:

1. Agreement of all parties;

2. A history of multi-employer collective bargaining; and

3. A desire on the part of the employer and (i) a rival union (the "petitioner") or (ii) an incumbent union (the "intervenor") to continue as a multi-employer unit.

An employer can withdraw from a multi-employer unit provided that:

1. The withdrawal is made prior to the date set by the collective bargaining agreement for modifications ("the window of opportunity"). For example, if the agreement expires on 4/30/02, and modifications are set for 3/31/02, an employer seeking to withdraw must serve notice of withdrawal before 3/31/02.

2. The withdrawal is made prior to the agreed-upon date for collective bargaining negotiations set in the CBA.

3. The withdrawal is unequivocal.

Once negotiations begin, withdrawal is not allowed unless there is mutual consent or some unusual circumstance, e.g., financial pressure. The reason for this requirement is a concern that if the employer could withdraw during negotiations, it would undermine the good faith bargaining process and negatively impact labor stability.

The Board has held that a union has the same right as an employer to withdraw from multi-employer unit bargaining. The Board reasoned that there is no basis for treating a union differently in this regard, and an inequality of freedom to withdraw would cause friction and instability in the bargaining unit. Further, the Board reasoned that unions would be reluctant to initiate multi-employer bargaining if the decision to do so would be irrevocable.

WORK ASSIGNMENT DISPUTES

Section 8(b)(4)(D) of the NLRA prohibits unions from: (i) forcing or requiring an employer to assign particular work to employees in a particular labor organization over another union (the "object"); and (ii) picketing (the "means").

Such a problem may arise when, for example, an employer is faced with a dispute involving two unions. The employer may file a charge with the Board for guidance. The Board orders what is known as a Section 10(k) proceeding unless the two unions come to some agreement within 10 days after notice of the filing of the charge.

Voluntary Resolution of Dispute

As a practical matter, unions prefer to resolve matters between themselves if possible rather than involving the Board. To avoid the Section 10(k) proceeding the unions may:

1. Voluntarily resolve the matter through:

    (i) The National Joint Board for settlement of jurisdictional disputes—an arbitration panel; or

    (ii) The AFL-CIO constitutional machinery. However, employers are not bound since they are not parties to the AFL-CIO constitution.

2. Reach an agreement that one union can prevail this time and the other union will prevail in the next dispute.

Section 10(k) Proceeding

If the parties cannot voluntarily resolve the dispute, the Section 10(k) proceeding is held. The Board looks at certain factors to determine who will get the disputed work. It applies a balancing test which includes an analysis of the following factors:

1. The collective bargaining agreements in the area and industry, including those between these unions, and with this employer, etc.;

2. Industry and area practice;

3. Past practice with the employer;

4. Agreements between international unions or rival unions; and

5. Joint Board decisions. However, these decisions are not binding.

If the Board awards one union the work and the other union doesn't comply, the Board cannot go into court to enforce the award because it is not a final order. In that case, the Board must issue a "cease and desist" order pursuant to section 8(b)(4), which is enforceable.

Temporary Restraining Orders

The Board can get a temporary restraining order (TRO) from the Court under Section 10(l) prior to the Section 10(k) proceeding, however, there is no mandate to obtain the TRO. It is at the Board's discretion whether to do so, and based on whether or not the Board believes the employer's charge is true. The purpose of the TRO is to restore the status quo so that a neutral arbiter can help resolve the matter.

CHAPTER 5:
COLLECTIVE BARGAINING

THE DUTY TO BARGAIN

Section 8(d) of the FLRA requires an employer and the representative of its employees to meet at reasonable times, to confer in good faith about certain matters, and to put into writing any agreement reached if requested by either party. The parties must confer in good faith with respect to wages, hours, and other terms or conditions of employment, the negotiation of an agreement, or any question arising under an agreement.

These obligations are imposed equally on the employer and the representative of its employees. This obligation does not, however, compel either party to agree to a proposal by the other, nor does it require either party to make a concession to the other.

Pursuant to Sections 8(a)(5) and 8(b)(3) of the NLRA, it is an unfair labor practice for either the employer or the certified union to refuse to bargain in good faith:

> Section 8(a)(5) states that "It shall be an unfair labor practice for an employer to refuse to bargain collectively with the representatives of his employees, subject to the provisions of Section 9(a)."

> Section 8(b)(3) of the Act provides that "It shall be an unfair labor practice for a labor organization . . . to refuse to bargain collectively with an employer provided it is the representative of its employees."

Section 8(b)(3) was added to force unions to also bargain in good faith collectively because otherwise a union could have a "take it or leave it" approach and break the employer economically.

Thus, the duty to bargain in good faith is a mutual duty between the union and the employer. The purpose is to promote industrial peace. The requirement to bargain in good faith has been interpreted to mean that the parties are obligated to meet and discuss terms, but that they are not required to come to an agreement.

In reality, collective bargaining involves a power struggle between labor and management. Economic weapons are used before, during and after

---

the bargaining process by both sides to try and force the other side to give in to its demands. Both sides must carefully consider their options. The union must consider whether it can afford to take its employees out on strike and subject them to a possible lockout. On the other hand, the employer must consider whether it can afford a strike or lockout.

It is recognized that the parties must be given great latitude during negotiations, without government intrusion into substantive matters. It is not the role of the Board to regulate the "weapons" used as part of this negotiation system. If so, the Board would be able to influence the substantive terms of the agreement.

For example, economic pressure is not inconsistent with good faith bargaining. There is a balance of power, and it is not the Board's responsibility to equalize that power. If an economic weapon is taken away from a union, the employer is made more powerful, and vice-versa.

THE COLLECTIVE BARGAINING AGREEMENT

A collective bargaining agreement generally sets forth:

1. The wages, hours, benefits and conditions of employment;
2. The type of work the bargaining units perform; and
3. Grievance procedures.

A collective bargaining agreement guarantees work stability. An employee cannot be fired without "just cause." This contrasts with "at will" employment where an employee can be fired for any reason other than those prohibited by law, such as discrimination or the exercise of an employee's Section 7 rights.

A collective bargaining agreement affords an employee more protection because there are informal methods of dispute resolution available without having to take the matter directly to Court. The union, as the employee's representative, is under an obligation to represent the rights of the employee. This is known as the duty of fair representation. If a union breaches that duty, a lawsuit can be brought by the employee against the union.

THE CONTRACT BAR

A valid, written collective bargaining agreement of definite duration bars an election sought by an outside union for the length of the agreement, up to a maximum of 3 years. An agreement which extends beyond 3 years is unenforceable to the extent it exceeds 3 years. This is known as the "contract bar doctrine."

A representative petition by a rival union can be filed between 90 to 60 days prior to the expiration of the agreement (the "window of opportunity"). Thereafter, no new representation petitions can be filed (the "insulation period"). Contracts with no set duration have no bar effect at all. An untimely election petition will be dismissed.

The union and the employer are the parties to the collective bargaining agreement, thus, they are the only ones who can go to Court to enforce its provisions.

For example, a collective bargaining agreement may contain an absolute no-strike provision. If an employer breaches a term of the collective bargaining agreement, the employees are not permitted to strike in retaliation. However, the employer's breach of the agreement is still a Section 8(a)(1) and (3) violation, and the employees do have some recourse.

In general, there are three ways to proceed when an employer breaches a term of the collective bargaining agreement:

1. A charge may be brought against the employer with the Board for interference with the employees' Section 7 rights. The Board can issue a "cease and desist" order.

2. If the collective bargaining agreement provides for arbitration, this may be a cheaper and faster method of resolving the dispute. The judgment is binding. The only way to overturn an arbitrator's award on appeal is to find fraud or illegality.

3. Section 301 of the LMRA gives District Courts jurisdiction over suits involving collective bargaining agreements only.

Once a collective bargaining agreement expires, the employees can go out on strike. Therefore, negotiations for a new collective bargaining agreement usually start prior to its expiration.

Exclusions to the Contract Bar

Notwithstanding the foregoing, not every contract will bar an election. Examples of contracts that would not bar an election include the following:

1. The contract is not in writing, or is not signed.

2. The contract has not been ratified by the members or the union, if such is expressly required.

3. The contract does not contain substantial terms or conditions of employment sufficient to stabilize the bargaining relationship.

4. The contract can be terminated by either party at any time for any reason.

5. The contract contains a clearly illegal union-security clause.

6. The bargaining unit is not appropriate.

7. The union that entered the contract with the employer is no longer in existence or is unable or unwilling to represent the employees.

8. The contract discriminates between employees on racial grounds.

9. The contract covers union members only.

10. The contracting union is involved in a basic internal conflict at the highest levels with resulting unstabilizing confusion about the identity of the union.

11. The employer's operations have changed substantially since the contract was executed.

GRIEVANCE PROCEDURES

A collective bargaining agreement may provide for a variety of remedies in handling grievances. Depending upon the particular offense, the agreement usually sets forth a system of progressive discipline, e.g., verbal warning, written warning, suspension, dismissal.

Grievance proceedings generally begin with a number of steps taken at the in-house level. These steps may range from informal to formal proceedings. The employee and shop steward will first discuss the problem with the immediate supervisor. If the problem is not resolved at that level, it is usually brought through the chain of command until all in-house resources are exhausted.

If the problem cannot be resolved in-house, the next step usually called for in the collective bargaining agreement is grievance arbitration. If either party to the agreement refuses to submit the grievance to arbitration, the other party may be able to compel submission through litigation at the federal or state court level.

The arbitration proceeding is not as formal as a court proceeding. The arbitrator hears the evidence and generally issues a written opinion and award. If the losing party does not abide by the arbitration decision, the prevailing party retains the right to enforce the arbitrator's award in court. However, the non-complying party is usually prohibited from arguing the facts if the prevailing party is forced to seek enforcement at that level.

EMPLOYER CONTRACTS

When employees are not represented by a union, the employer has complete control over the terms and conditions of employment. Most jurisdictions have employment "at will." This means that the employer may fire an employee with or without cause, provided the dismissal does not violate a statute, e.g. discrimination. An employer is also free to enter into contracts with its employees concerning the terms and conditions of employment.

When the employees are represented by a union, the employer must negotiate with that union and cannot undermine the collective bargaining agreement by granting terms which conflict with the collective bargaining agreement. Although an employer is still permitted to enter into individual contracts with its employees, those contracts are subsidiary to the collective bargaining agreement.

For example, in a 1944 case, *J.I. Case Co. v. NLRB*, the employer had contracts with 75 percent of its employees which provided for items such as pay raises, etc. The contracts were not a condition of employment and were valid for one-year terms. No coercion was used and the employer committed no unfair labor practices.

While the contracts were still in effect, the CIO petitioned the Board for certification of bargaining units at the Company. The CIO sought exclusive representation of the unit. A hearing was held, and the Company claimed that the contracts were a bar to the certification proceeding. The Board directed an election and the CIO won. A unit was certified which included all production and maintenance employees.

The CIO asked the employer to bargain but the Company refused to negotiate any of the terms contained in the existing contracts. It said it would negotiate on other matters, and would negotiate on the remaining issues once the existing contracts expired.

The CIO filed an unfair labor practice charge. The Board held that the Company violated Section 8(a)(5) for refusing to bargain with the union. The Board ordered the Company to cease enforcing the existing contracts and to bargain with the union. The Circuit Court of Appeals granted an enforcement order, and certiorari to the U.S. Supreme Court was sought.

Upon appeal, the Board's order was affirmed. The Supreme Court held that the individual contracts were subsidiary to the collective bargaining agreement with the union, but that there was no bar to employee contracts which govern issues not covered by the collective bargaining agreement.

Thus, an employer can enter into an individual contract with its employees, but it must be able to coexist with the collective bargaining agreement. If there is a conflict, the collective bargaining agreement prevails.

discouraging membership in a labor organization. Thus, the Act makes it illegal for an employer to discriminate in employment because of an employee's union activity within the protection of the Act. Examples of violations of Section 8(a)(3) include:

1. Discharging employees because they urged other employees to join a union.

2. Refusing to reinstate employees when jobs they are qualified for are open because they took part in a union's lawful strike.

3. Granting of "superseniority" to those hired to replace employees engaged in a lawful strike.

4. Demoting employees because they circulated a union petition among other employees asking the employer for an increase in pay.

5. Discontinuing an operation at one plant and discharging the employees involved followed by opening the same operation at another plant with new employees because the employees at the first plant joined a union.

6. Refusing to hire qualified applicants for jobs because they belong to a union. It would also be a violation if the qualified applicants were refused employment because they did not belong to a union, or because they belonged to one union rather than another.

Notwithstanding the above, the Act does not limit an employer's right to discharge, transfer, or layoff an employee for genuine economic reasons or for such good cause as disobedience or bad work. This right applies equally to employees who are active in support of a union and to those who are not.

In *Budd Co. v. NLRB* (1943), the CIO filed a charge that the Budd Co. committed an unfair labor practice under Sections 8(a)(1), (2) and (3) when it discharged an employee because he engaged in union activities on behalf of the CIO. The Budd Co. had created its own company union—the "Budd Association." The Budd Co. argued that it discharged the employee for misconduct. Following a hearing, the Board ordered disestablishment of the "Budd Association" and reinstatement of the employee.

On appeal, the Court of Appeals affirmed and held that there was enough evidence to show that the employee was actually fired for his effort to unionize.

Discrimination for NLRB Activity

Section 8(a)(4) makes it an unfair labor practice for an employer "to discharge or otherwise discriminate against an employee because he has filed charges or given testimony under this Act." This provision guards the right of employees to seek the protection of the Act by using the processes of the NLRB. Examples of violations of Section 8(a)(4) include:

1. Refusing to reinstate employees when jobs they are otherwise qualified for are open because they filed charges with the NLRB claiming their layoffs were based on union activity.

2. Demoting employees because they testified at an NLRB hearing.

Refusal to Bargain in Good Faith

Section 8(a)(5) makes it illegal for an employer to refuse to bargain in good faith about wages, hours, and other conditions of employment with the representative selected by a majority of the employees in a unit appropriate for collective bargaining. A bargaining representative which seeks to enforce its right concerning an employer under this section must show that it has been designated by a majority of the employees, that the unit is appropriate, and that there has been both a demand that the employer bargain and a refusal by the employer to do so.

No-Solicitation Rules

Solicitation by Employee Union Organizers

In *Republic Aviation v. NLRB* (1945), the Board struck down a "no-solicitation of any type" rule adopted by the Company prior to any attempt an unionization. In this case, an employee was discharged for violating the rule when he solicited union membership on his own time.

The Board held that the no-solicitation rule violated Section 8(a)(1) and (3) of the NLRA because it interfered with Section 7 rights and discriminated against employees. The Board (i) entered a cease and desist order; (ii) ordered reinstatement of the employee; and (iii) ordered a rescission of the no-solicitation rule insofar as it prohibited union activity during an employee's own time.

On appeal, both the Circuit Court of Appeals and the U.S. Supreme Court affirmed, holding that the test is "working time vs. non-working time."

Thus, a no-solicitation rule is presumed valid during working hours—i.e., while the employee is actually engaged in work. There is a presumption of validity absent evidence that the rule was adopted out of anti-union bias. The no-solicitation rule is presumed invalid during an employee's non-working hours. Employers cannot prohibit solicitation during non-working hours, even on company property, unless necessary to maintain production or discipline. A company must overcome this presumption in order to adopt a no-solicitation rule during non-working hours.

Therefore, if an employer violates the Act, and an employee is fired because of it, that discharge is invalid. For example, if an employer adopts a "no-solicitation during nonworking hours rule," and then fires an employee for violating the rule, the discharge is invalid because the underlying rule itself was invalid and violated the Act.

Solicitation by Non-Employee Union Organizers

An employer may validly prohibit the distribution of union literature by non-employees on company property provided:

1. Reasonable methods by the union through other methods of communication would enable the union to reach the employees with the same message.

2. There can be no discrimination by denying access to unions and not others. For example, if non-employees are permitted to sell cookies on company property, then non-employees should also be able to conduct unionization drives.

3. When the inaccessibility of the employees makes the unionizing efforts of the non-employees ineffective because they are unable to reach employees through the alternate usual channels, then the employer's right to exclude non-employee union organizers from company property yields to the employee's Section 7 rights under the Act. An example of such inaccessibility is a so-called "company town" where the employees work and live within the company's property.

In *NLRB v. Babcock* (1956), a company adopted a "no-distribution" rule, refusing to permit the distribution of union literature by non-employee union organizers on company-owned parking lots. The union filed a charge. The Board ruled that this policy violated Section 8(a)(1) of the NLRA even though it applied to non-employees, reasoning that it would be hard for the organizers to reach the employees off the parking lot.

The Board ordered the company to rescind its no-distribution rule. The Company refused to comply and the Board sought enforcement in the Court of Appeals. The Court of Appeals refused to impose servitude on the employer's property for non-employees, holding that it is the employees—not the union—that has the right to enforce Section 7 rights.

The U.S. Supreme Court granted certiorari and reversed with instructions to the Board on how to apply the law. It held that a company may adopt a no-distribution rule prohibiting distribution of union literature by non-employees provided: (i) the union has other means to reach the employees; and (ii) the rule is not discriminatory in that it is not targeted at unions only. Nevertheless, the Court held that if there was no other means of organizing, then non-employee union organizers had the right to communicate with the employees to the extent necessary.

In the *Babcock* case, the no-distribution rule was upheld under the Supreme Court test because the employees were found to be otherwise accessible—e.g., (i) by mail; (ii) by telephone; (iii) by drive-by access; and (iv) in-town access.

Thus, the greater the degree of inaccessibility, the more likely the Board will allow non-employees to unionize on company property. The underlying policy with this reasoning is to encourage the employees to undertake the union organizing.

Speech Rules

An employer is prohibited from making a pre-election speech on company time to mass audiences within 24 hours before an election. The Courts have held that this "poisons the well" for a fair election. Thus, if objections are thereafter filed, the election can be thrown out. However, speeches are permissible when given on an employee's own time, with voluntary attendance. Distribution of literature, however, is generally permissible at any time.

Coercive Interrogation

The Board has held that interrogation by an employer is considered coercive if:

1. It has no valid purpose;

2. There is no communication of the purpose; and

3. There is no assurance that there will be no reprisals.

In *NLRB v. Lorben Corp*, the AFL-CIO filed a charge against the company alleging that, following the discharge of an employee for union activities, the president's solicitation of ballots to the employees concerning their desire for union representation was prohibited coercive interrogation.

The Board found that the employer's action had no legitimate purpose, and failed to assure the employees that there would be no reprisals. However, the Court of Appeals refused to enforce the Board's order, finding that the employer was not coercive or intimidating, and that the interrogation was not unlawful per se.

Although the Board does not consider itself bound by Court of Appeals decisions, the Court set forth a more comprehensive test than that used by the Board to determine whether there has been coercive interrogation, including a review of: (i) the background of the employer/employee relations and history of employer hostility and discrimination; (ii) the nature of the information sought (e.g. targeting individuals); (iii) the identity of the interrogator (e.g., what position he or she holds in the company); (iv) the place and method of interrogation (e.g., in the office); and (v) the truthfulness of the reply.

Subsequently, in *NLRB v. Struksnes Corp.*, the Board restated its *Lorben* rule, holding that absent unusual circumstances, the polling of employees violates Section 8(a)(1) unless:

1. The purpose of the poll is to determine the truth of the union's claim to a majority, which is the only valid purpose to poll;

2. The purpose is communicated to the employees;

3. There are assurances against reprisals;

4. Secret ballots are used; and

5. The employer has not engaged in unfair labor practices or coercive behavior in the past.

Conferring Economic Benefits on Employees Prior to Election

In *NLRB v. Exchange Parts Co.* (1964), the Board held that it was an unfair labor practice in violation of Section 8(a)(1) when an employer conferred economic benefits—e.g. holiday pay, pay raises, vacations, etc.—on its employees shortly before a union election. The election was held and the union lost although it had previously determined that a majority of the employees wanted unionization.

The Board reasoned that such benefits induced the employees to vote against the union. The Court of Appeals denied enforcement holding that since the economic changes were permanent, there was no unfair labor practice. The Supreme Court reversed on appeal, holding that:

1. Conferring economic benefits pre-election does interfere with the right to organize;

2. Section 8(a)(1) provides for the right for employees to organize without employer interference;

3. Employer shouldn't engage in such activities during an election or during the period of union organization;

4. There will be a presumption that an unfair labor practice occurred because there is an implied threat;

5. It is an unfair labor practice for an employer to buy votes; and

6. Employers can confer economic benefits on its employees at any other time.

Closing Down the Business

In *Textile Workers Union v. Darlington Co.*, the Board found that Darlington Co.—one of a group of textile mills owned and controlled by Milliken Corp.—had committed an unfair labor practice when it permanently closed its plant following an election. The Darlington Co. had vigorously opposed unionization in its shop and had threatened to close the plant if a union was elected.

When the union was elected, it followed through on its threat. The union filed a charge but the company contended that it had to close because it could no longer compete. The Board held that, based on the prior threat to close, the closing was in fact due to anti-union bias in violation of Section 8(a)(3) of the Act.

The Board ordered backpay for the employees until they were hired either in (i) equal positions or (ii) by another Milliken plant. The Board further determined the Milliken plants to be one single integrated employer, and ordered that the employer bargain with the union. The Court of Appeals refused to enforce the Board's order, holding that the company had the right to close all or part of its business.

The U.S. Supreme Court vacated the Court of Appeals ruling, holding that an employer has the right to close all of the business, but not a part of the business. The Court reasoned that complete liquidation yields no future benefits, if bona fide. Termination of the entire business, even if discriminatory, ends the employer/employee relationship because there are no more employees. However, partial closing gives the employer leverage over any remaining employees.

Thus, the Court agreed in part with the Court of Appeals that if Darlington Co. was an independent employer, it could legally liquidate its business. However, if Darlington was part of the Milliken Corp., the remedy would be to reinstate the discharged employees in other parts of the business.

On remand, the Board used the following factors to determine whether there was a single employer ("Milliken"), and if the closing was an unfair labor practice:

1. Whether the employer had an interest in another business run by the same employer upon which the effect of closing will benefit it by discouraging unionism in that other business;

2. Whether the employer acted with the purpose of producing this chilling effect on unionism at the other business; and

3. Whether the result was foreseeable.

After applying the above test, the Board found that the criteria was met and the Board's order was renewed and enforced.

Nevertheless, if a company can demonstrate that its closing is based on factual economic reasons, there would be no violation provided there are no threats made to the employees.

UNFAIR LABOR PRACTICES BY UNIONS

Union Conduct Impairing Right to Organize

As set forth in Section 8(b)(1)(A) of the NLRA, it is an unfair labor practice for a union "to restrain or coerce employees in the exercise of the rights guaranteed in Section 7." Section 7 is not, however, intended to impair the rights of a labor organization to prescribe its own membership rules.

Section 8(b)(1)(A) is similar to Section 8(a)(1) in that it may be violated independently by conduct that restrains or coerces employees in the exercise of their Section 7 rights regardless of whether the conduct also violates other provisions of Section 8(b). However, unlike Section 8(a), violations of the other provisions of Section 8(b), in general—i.e., 8(b)(2)-8(b)(7)—do not derivatively violate Section 8(b)(1)(A).

Examples of restraint or coercion by a union that violate Section 8(b)(1)(A) include:

1. Mass picketing in such numbers that nonstriking employees are physically barred from entering the plant.

2. Acts of force or violence on the picket line, or in connection with a strike.

3. Threats to do bodily injury to nonstriking employees.

4. Threats to employees that they will lose their jobs unless they support the union's activities.

5. Statement to employees who oppose the union that the employees will lose their jobs if the union wins a majority in the plant.

6. Entering into an agreement with an employer that recognizes the union as exclusive bargaining representative when it has not been chosen by a majority of the employees.

7. Fining or expelling members for crossing a picket line that is unlawful under the Act or that violates a no-strike agreement.

8. Fining employees for crossing a picket line after they resigned from the union.

9. Fining or expelling members for filing unfair labor practice charges with the Board or for participating in an investigation conducted by the Board.

In addition, examples of restraint or coercion that violate Section 8(b)(1)(A) when committed by a union that is the exclusive bargaining representative include:

1. Refusing to process a grievance in retaliation against an employee's criticism of union officers.

2. Maintaining a seniority arrangement with an employer under which seniority is based on the employee's prior representation by the union elsewhere.

3. Rejecting an application for referral to a job in a unit represented by the union based on the applicant's race or union activities.

Restraint and Coercion of Employers

Section 8(b)(1)(B) of the Act prohibits a labor organization from restraining or coercing an employer in the selection of a bargaining representative. The prohibition applies regardless of whether the labor organization is the majority representative of the employees in the bargaining unit and extends to coercion applied by a union to a union member who is a representative of the employer in the adjustment of grievances.

Examples of violations of Section 8(b)(1)(B) include:

1. Insisting on meeting only with a company's owners and refusing to meet with the attorney the company has engaged to represent the company in contract negotiations, and threatening to strike to force the company to accept its demands.

2. Striking members of an employer association that bargains with the union as the representative of the employers to compel the struck employers to sign individual contracts with the union.

3. Insisting during contract negotiations that the employer agree to accept working conditions that will be established by a bargaining group to which it does not belong.

4. Fining or expelling supervisors for the way they apply the bargaining contract while carrying out their supervisory functions or for crossing a picket line during a strike to perform their supervisory duties.

Causing or Attempting to Cause Discrimination

Section 8(b)(2) makes it an unfair labor practice for a labor organization to cause an employer to discriminate against an employee in violation of Section 8(a)(3).

Examples of violations of Section 8(b)(2) include:

1. Causing an employer to discharge employees because they circulated a petition urging a change in the union's method of selecting shop stewards.

2. Causing an employer to discharge employees because they made speeches against a contract proposed by the union.

3. Making a contract that requires an employer to hire only members of the union or employees "satisfactory" to the union.

4. Causing an employer to reduce employees' seniority because they engaged in antiunion acts.

5. Refusing referral or giving preference on the basis of race or union activities in making job referrals to units represented by the union.

6. Seeking the discharge of an employee under a union-security agreement for failure to pay a fine levied by the union.

Refusal to Bargain in Good Faith

Section 8(b)(3) makes it illegal for a labor organization to refuse to bargain in good faith with an employer about wages, hours, and other conditions of employment if it is the representative of that employer's employees.

Examples of violations of Section 8(b)(3) include:

1. Insisting on the inclusion of illegal provisions in a contract, such as a closed shop or a discriminatory hiring hall.

2. Refusing to negotiate on a proposal for a written contract.

3. Striking against an employer who has bargained, and continues to bargain, on a multiemployer basis to compel it to bargain separately.

4. Refusing to meet with the attorney designated by the employer as its representative in negotiations.

5. Terminating an existing contract and striking for a new one without notifying the employer, the Federal Mediation and Conciliation Service, and the state mediation service, if any.

6. Conditioning the execution of an agreement on inclusion of a nonmandatory provision such as a performance bond.

7. Refusing to process a grievance because of the race, sex, or union activities of an employee for whom the union is the statutory bargaining representative.

Prohibited Strikes and Boycotts

Section 8(b)(4) prohibits a labor organization from engaging in strikes or boycotts or taking other specified actions to accomplish certain objectives. For example, under Section 8(b)(4)(A), a union may not induce or encourage a strike, work stoppage or boycott, or use coercion to compel an employer or self-employed person to join any labor or employer organization or to force an employer to enter a hot cargo agreement prohibited by Section 8(e).

Pursuant to Section 8(b)(4)(B), a union cannot compel recognition of an uncertified union. This section contains the Act's "secondary boycott" prohibition. For example, a secondary boycott occurs if a union has a dispute with Company A (the "primary employer") and, in furtherance of that dispute, causes the employees of Company B (the "secondary employer") to stop handling the products of Company A, or otherwise forces Company B to stop doing business with Company A. The Act prohibits both the secondary boycott and the threat of it.

Nevertheless, the prohibitions of Section 8(b)(4)(B) do not protect a secondary employer from the "incidental" effects of union action that is taken directly against the primary employe, e.g., it is lawful for a union to urge employees of a secondary supplier at the primary employer's plant not to cross a picket line at the primary employer's site.

Notwithstanding the foregoing, the secondary employer has to be in a neutral position in the dispute between the union and the primary employer or the secondary employer will not be protected under the Act. If so, the secondary employer will be considered an "ally" of the primary employer.

Excessive or Discriminatory Membership Fees

Section 8(b)(5) makes it illegal for a union to charge employees who are covered by an authorized union-security agreement a membership fee "in an amount which the Board finds excessive or discriminatory under all the circumstances."

Featherbedding

Section 8(b)(6) forbids a labor organization "to cause or attempt to cause an employer to pay or deliver or agree to pay or deliver any money or other thing of value, in the nature of an exaction, for services which are not performed or not to be performed." This unlawful practice is known as "featherbedding."

Featherbedding is basically defined as an unfair labor practice whereby the time spent, or number of employees needed, to complete a particular task, is increased unnecessarily for the purpose of creating employment. However, although a union is prohibited from causing an employer to pay for services not performed, if the work is performed, even if the services are basically useless to the employer, this is not a violation of Section 8(b)(6).

For example, in *American Newspaper Association v. NLRB* (1953), technology was reducing the available work for the printer employees of a publishing company. The collective bargaining agreement required the employer to pay the printers for setting type which had already been set on a permanent mat. This practice was known as "setting bogus." The reset type was then discarded.

The Company brought a charge that the practice was illegal under the anti-featherbedding statute. The Board held that "setting bogus" was not an unfair labor practice under the law because the employees did perform the work. The Board left the question of "worth of service" up to the parties. The Supreme Court affirmed and dismissed the charge.

Legislative history shows that the anti-featherbedding statute was meant to prohibit the practice of exacting money for services not performed or not to be performed. An example of a featherbedding unfair labor practice would occur if a musician's union forces an employer to pay a minimum of 10 musicians for a session, when there is only room for 6 musicians to actually perform.

Organizational and Recognitional Picketing by Noncertified Unions

Section 8(b)(7) prohibits a labor organization that is not currently certified as the employees' representative from picketing or threatening to picket with an object of obtaining recognition by the employer ("recognitional picketing") or acceptance by his employees as their representative ("organizational picketing"). The object of picketing is ascertained from all the surrounding facts including the message on the picket signs and any communications between the union and the employer.

"Recognitional" picketing as used in Section 8(b)(7) refers to picketing to obtain an employer's initial recognition of the union as bargaining representative of its employees or to force the employer, without formal recognition of the union, to maintain a specific and detailed set of working conditions. It does not include picketing by an incumbent union for continued recognition or for a new contract.

Recognitional and organizational picketing are prohibited in three specific instances:

1. When the employer has lawfully recognized another union and a representation election would be barred by either the provisions of the Act or the Board's Rules.

2. When a valid NLRB representation election has been held within the previous 12 months.

3. When a representation petition is not filed "within a reasonable period of time not to exceed thirty days from the commencement of such picketing."

Conferring Economic Benefits on Employees Prior to Election

In *NLRB v. Savair Manufacturing Co.*, the U.S. Supreme Court affirmed the Court of Appeals ruling which denied enforcement of a Board Order directing the Company to bargain with a union following election. As in the above-referenced *Exchange Parts* case involving an employer conferring economic benefits prior to the election, the Court found that the union had also "poisoned the well."

Prior to the election, the union circulated recognition slips to the employees, advising that those who signed prior to certification would not have to pay the initiation fee. The employees were not told how high the initiation fee would be. The Court found that this action had a powerful coercive effect on the employees, and presented a false representation of employee support for the union. The underlying concern is that unions would be able to "buy" the 30 percent support needed to get an election.

HOT CARGO AGREEMENTS

Section 8(e) of the FLRA, added to the Act in 1959, makes it an unfair labor practice for any labor organization and any employer to enter into what is commonly called a "hot cargo" or "hot goods" agreement. It may also limit the restrictions that can be placed on the subcontracting of work by an employer. Section 8(e) specifically forbids any labor organization and any employer to enter into any contract or agreement, express or implied, whereby the employer ceases or refrains or agrees to cease or refrain from handling, using, selling, transporting, or otherwise dealing in any of the products of any other employer.

Prior to the 1959 amendment, hot cargo clauses were common in the trucking and construction industries. A typical clause provided that employees would not be required by their employer to handle or work on goods going to, or coming from, an employer designated by the union as "unfair." Such goods were said to be "hot cargo." These clauses were most common in the construction and trucking industries.

Pursuant to Section 8(e) of the Act, any contract entered into by an employer and a labor union whereby the employer agrees to stop doing business with any other employer is void and unenforceable, and any union action, or the threat of it, to force an employer to agree to a hot cargo provision has been held by the Board to be a violation of Section 8(b)(4). There is a special ULP charge form which addresses this situation.

A sample NLRB Unfair Labor Practice Charge Form pursuant to Section 8(e) is set forth at Appendix 9.

PROCEDURAL STEPS IN FILING AN ULP CHARGE CASE

When an unfair labor practice is alleged, the aggrieved party files what is known as a charge case with the Board. The party filing the charge is called the "charging party." The employer or union against whom the charge is filed is called the "charged party."

A charge case may be filed by a union, an employer or an employee. The "charge" generally accuses the employer or union of engaging in an unfair labor practice. The charge is then filed and investigated by a field examiner. The appropriate field office conducts an investigation to determine whether there is reasonable cause to believe an unfair labor practice has occurred. Witness statements and other necessary evidence are secured upon which to decide the charge.

Among other things, the charging party must be prepared to provide details of necessary events, including dates, times, places and names of witnesses. The charging party may be requested to provide additional evidence or information as the investigation progresses.

The charged party will be requested to provide relevant information and, if the evidence warrants, will be asked to make its witnesses available for an interview. The charged party may be requested to provide additional evidence and/or information as the investigation progresses. Parties may be asked to submit their legal arguments. A decision will be rendered following a thorough and complete investigation.

Once the investigation is completed, a decision will be made as to whether the case has merit. The length of time it takes to decide whether a case has merit may vary depending upon: (i) the Board's case load; (ii) the distance between the Board's office and the site of the dispute; (iii) the priority of the case; (iv) the number of witnesses to be interviewed; and (v) the complexity of the legal and factual issues raised.

The Board will evaluate cases to determine whether they should seek an injunction to stop the alleged unfair labor practices temporarily until a decision is rendered.

A sample ULP charge form against an employer is set forth at Appendix 10, and a sample ULP charge form against a labor organization is set forth at Appendix 11.

Opportunity for Withdrawal or Waiver

If the Regional Director decides that the charge has no merit, the reasons will be explained to the charging party and the Board will offer the charging party an opportunity to withdraw the charge. If the charging party prefers, the Regional Director will dismiss the charge, with or without detailed reasons at the charging party's request, and the charging party can appeal. The dismissal letter will tell the charging party how to file such an appeal.

A sample charge withdrawal request is set forth at Appendix 12.

According to NLRB statistics, from the time a charge is first filed, in cases found to have no merit, a withdrawal will be approved or a dismissal letter will issue within 7 to 15 weeks in the majority of cases. If the charging party appeals the dismissal to the General Counsel's Office of Appeals in Washington, a decision will be issued within 60 days from the date the appeal is received by the Office of Appeals in a majority of cases.

Cases involving very complex facts and/or novel or difficult legal issues, or remands to the Regional Offices for further investigation, may take longer. According to NLRB statistics, approximately 65 percent of all unfair labor practice charges are dismissed or voluntarily withdrawn for lack of merit following an investigation.

The losing party may waive their right to request a review of the decision or to file exceptions.

A sample review request waiver form is set forth at Appendix 13.

Settlement

If the charge has merit, the charged party will be offered an opportunity to settle before a formal complaint is issued. According to the NLRB, from the time a charge is first filed, a complaint, settlement or adjustment should be expected within 7 to 15 weeks in the majority of cases. According to NLRB statistics, of the total charges filed each year—estimated to be about 35,000—approximately one-third are found to have merit, and of that one-third, over 90 percent are settled.

Trial

If settlement efforts fail, a formal complaint is issued and the case goes to a hearing. The parties will continue to try to settle the case even after issuance of the complaint. If the case cannot be settled and proceeds to trial, a Board attorney will prepare and present the case to the administrative law judge.

Other parties to the case may be present, be represented by counsel if they so choose, and may examine witnesses and present relevant evidence. The length of time before trial will vary depending on a number of factors, including how many other cases are set for trial.

After the trial is concluded, the judge will issue a written decision and recommended order, which can be appealed to the Board in Washington and ultimately to the federal courts. The length of time until decisions of the judge and the Board issue will vary depending on a number of factors, including the length of the trial and the complexity of the issues.

According to the NLRB, in the majority of all cases heard by a judge, the decision will issue in less than 4 months. In the majority of all cases decided by the Board, the Board's decision will issue in less than 4 months.

After the judge gives the Board a decision, it allows a period of time for objections to be filed. If no objections are filed, the judge's decision generally becomes the Board's decision and it issues an order. If the Board's order is not followed, the case proceeds to the Circuit Court of Appeals for an enforcement order.

Board orders are enforced and reviewed in the Circuit Court of Appeals, and subject to further review by the U.S. Supreme Court on certiorari. Upon review, findings of fact by the Board are given great weight by the Circuit Court, but the way in which the law is applied to such facts is given lesser weight. There are often conflicts between the Board and the judicial system.

Injunctive Relief

Section 10(j) of the National Labor Relations Act empowers the NLRB to petition a federal district court for an injunction to temporarily prevent unfair labor practices by employers or unions and to restore the status quo, pending the full review of the case by the Board. In enacting this provision, Congress was concerned that delays inherent in the administrative processing of unfair labor practice charges, in certain instances, would frustrate the Act's remedial objectives.

In determining whether the use of Section 10(j) is appropriate in a particular case, the principal question is whether injunctive relief is necessary to preserve the Board's ability to effectively remedy the unfair labor practice alleged, and whether the alleged violator would otherwise reap the benefit from of its violation.

Under NLRB procedures, after deciding to issue an unfair labor practice complaint, the General Counsel may request authorization from the Board to seek injunctive relief. The Board votes on the General Counsel's request and, if a majority votes to authorize injunctive proceedings, the General Counsel files the case with an appropriate Federal district court.

In addition, Section 10(l) of the Act requires the Board to seek a temporary federal court injunction against certain forms of union misconduct, principally involving "secondary boycotts" and "recognitional picketing." Finally, under Section 10(e), the Board may ask a federal court of appeals to enjoin conduct that the Board has found to be unlawful.

The order, subject to appeal in the Court of Appeals, remains in effect while the Board fully adjudicates the merits of the unfair practice complaint or until the case is settled.

CHAPTER 7:
CONCERTED ACTIVITY

IN GENERAL

The use of economic pressure by both a union and an employer engaged in collective bargaining is an acceptable and legal tactic. For example, an employer may undertake what is known as a "lockout," as one such tactic. Lockouts are further discussed in this chapter.

Unions often engage in strikes, which are usually accompanied by picketing. The right to strike and picket are discussed in this chapter. Secondary boycotts—activities targeted at an employer other than the one with whom the union has a dispute—are prohibited under the NLRA. Secondary boycotts are also discussed in this chapter.

THE RIGHT TO STRIKE

Section 7 of the NLRA states, in part: "Employees shall have the right . . . to engage in other concerted activities for the purpose of collective bargaining or other mutual aid or protection." Strikes are included among these protected concerted activities. Section 13 also confers the right to strike: "Nothing in this Act, except as specifically provided for herein, shall be construed so as either to interfere with or impede or diminish in any way the right to strike, or to affect the limitations or qualifications on that right."

Nevertheless, the law does place limitations and qualifications on the right to strike. For example, the lawfulness of a strike may depend on the objective of the strike, on its timing, or on the conduct of the strikers.

Objective of Strike

Employees who strike for a lawful object fall into two classes "economic strikers" and "unfair labor practice strikers." Both classes continue as employees, but unfair labor practice strikers have greater rights of reinstatement to their jobs.

Economic Strikers

If the object of a strike is to obtain some economic concession from the employer, such as higher wages, shorter hours, or better working conditions, the striking employees are called economic strikers. They retain their status as employees and cannot be discharged, but they can be replaced by their employer. If the employer has hired bona fide permanent replacements who are filling the jobs of the economic strikers when the strikers apply unconditionally to go back to work, the strikers are not entitled to reinstatement at that time.

However, if the strikers do not obtain regular and substantially equivalent employment, they are entitled to be recalled to jobs for which they are qualified when openings in such jobs occur if they, or their bargaining representative, have made an unconditional request for their reinstatement.

Unfair Labor Practice Strikers

Employees who strike to protest an unfair labor practice committed by their employer are called unfair labor practice strikers. These strikers cannot be discharged or permanently replaced. When the strike ends, unfair labor practice strikers, absent serious misconduct on their part, are entitled to have their jobs back even if employees hired to do their work have to be discharged.

If the Board finds that economic strikers or unfair labor practice strikers who have made an unconditional request for reinstatement have been unlawfully denied reinstatement by their employer, the Board may award such strikers backpay starting at the time they should have been reinstated.

Timing of Strike

A strike may be unlawful because of its timing. For example, a strike that violates a no-strike provision of a contract is not protected by the Act, and the striking employees can be discharged or otherwise disciplined, unless the strike is called to protest certain kinds of unfair labor practices committed by the employer.

Conduct of Strikers

Strikers who engage in serious misconduct in the course of a strike may be refused reinstatement to their former jobs. This applies to both economic strikers and unfair labor practice strikers. Serious misconduct has been held to include, among other things, violence and threats of violence. Unlawful conduct by strikers may also include:

1. Physically blocking persons from entering or leaving a struck plant.

2. Threatening violence against nonstriking employees.

3. Attacking management representatives.

THE RIGHT TO PICKET

The right to picket is another form of concerted activity protected under Section 7 of the FLRA. However, picketing is also subject to limitations and qualifications. As with the right to strike, picketing can be prohibited because of its object or its timing, or misconduct on the picket line. For example, there may be restrictions concerning picketing on private property if it is determined that the union had alternative methods for public awareness. In addition, Section 8(b)(7) declares it to be an unfair labor practice for a union to picket for certain objects whether the picketing accompanies a strike or not.

Recognitional and Organizational Picketing

As discussed below, the rules concerning recognitional and organizational picketing differ according to whether a union is certified or non-certified.

Certified Union

A currently certified union may picket for recognition or organization for its members. It is not subject to the provisions of Section 8(b)(7) of the NLRA, which sets forth the rules governing organizational and recognitional picketing, as follows:

It shall be an unfair labor practice for a labor organization or its agents . . . to picket or cause to be picketed, or threaten to picket . . . any employer where the object thereof is forcing or requiring an employer to recognize or bargain with a labor organization as the representative of his employees, or forcing or requiring the employees of an employer to accept or select such labor organization as their collective bargaining representative, unless such labor organization is currently certified as the representative of such employees:

(A) where the employer has lawfully recognized . . . any other labor organization and a question concerning representation may not appropriately be raised under Section 9(e);

(B) where within the preceding 12 months a valid election under Section 9(c) . . . has been conducted (the "certification bar");

(C) where such picketing has been conducted without a petition under Section 9(c) being filed within a reasonable period of time not to exceed 30 days from the commencement of such picketing . . . provided . . . that nothing in paragraph (C) shall be construed to prohibit picketing or other publicity for the purpose of truthfully advising the public . . . unless an effect of such picketing is to induce any individual employed by any other person in the course of his employment, not to pick up, deliver or transport any goods or not to perform services. . .

Non-Certified Union

A non-certified union may not picket for recognition or organization:

1. Under Section 8(b)(7)(A), where there is (i) a lawfully recognized union representing the majority of employees; (ii) there is no proper question regarding representation under Section 9(c); and (iii) there exists a valid collective bargaining agreement during the contract bar period;

2. Under Section 8(b)(7)(B), where a valid election has been held in the past 12 months (the "election bar period");

3. Under Section 8(b)(7)(C), even where the union is not barred under Sections 8(b)(7)(A) or (B), picketing is limited to a period not exceeding 30 days unless a representation petition is filed prior to the expiration of the 30-day period.

Without such a representation petition, picketing beyond the 30-day period is an unfair labor practice. However, filing a timely representation petition "stays" the 30-day limitation and picketing may continue to the end of the petitioning process.

Expedited Election

In order to resolve questions concerning representation as quickly as possible, Congress has further shortened the picketing period set forth in Section 8(b)(7)(C) by providing for an "expedited election" under certain circumstances. However, expedited elections are applicable only in a Section 8(b)(7)(C) proceeding where a charge has been made that an unfair labor practice has occurred. If the employees designate the picketer as their bargaining union in the expedited election, the union is certified.

In the absence of such a ULP charge, the union cannot obtain an expedited election by merely engaging in organizational picketing and then filing a representation petition. Further, a picketing union may not obtain an expedited election merely because it files a representation petition pursuant to Section 8(b)(7)(C). In both scenarios, normal representation procedures are required, i.e. (i) a showing of substantial interest; and (ii) a Section 9(c)(1) pre-election hearing.

The expedited election procedures were devised to shield employers and employees from the adverse effects of prolonged recognitional/organizational picketing. Congress recognized that in order to promote uncoerced and free choices among the employees, there must be a balance of (i) the right of a union to picket versus (ii) their abuse of that right.

SECONDARY BOYCOTTS

Picketing is permissible at the primary employer's site, whether it takes place at the customer entrance or the employee/delivery entrance. Even if the picketing activity has the effect of keeping people away, it is still lawful. This is known as a "traditional boycott." A secondary boycott occurs when a union puts pressure on Employer "B" in order to get concessions from Employer "A."

Unfair Labor Practice

In 1947, under the Taft-Hartley Act, Section 8(b)(4)(A) was enacted to make specific kinds of secondary pressure an unfair labor practice. In 1959, under the Landrum-Griffin Act, Section 8(b)(4)(A) was merged into Section 8(b)(4)(B), providing that:

> It shall be an unfair labor practice for a labor organization or its agents . . . (i) to engage in, induce or encourage any individual employed by any person . . . to engage in a strike . . . refuse to perform services . . . or (ii) to threaten, coerce or restrain any person . . . where in either case an object thereof is . . . forcing or requiring any person to cease . . . dealing in the products of another producer . . . or to cease doing business with any other person . . . provided that nothing contained in this clause shall be construed to make unlawful . . . any primary strike or primary picketing.

This section makes it illegal to seek to achieve certain objects through the use of certain means. In order for an unfair labor practice to exist, both a proscribed means and a proscribed object must be present. For example, the proscribed "means" may be striking, picketing or making threats. The proscribed "object" may be forcing the employer to join a union or enter into an agreement to engage in a secondary boycott.

Permissible Picketing Activities

Unions are free to:

1. Picket the primary;

2. Engage in putting pressure on secondaries; and

3. In the course of picketing, to persuade customers, delivery persons, and others not to do business with the primary.

A union cannot, however, encourage the secondary employer's employees to strike their employer. This would constitute an unfair labor practice. Thus, picketing is not permissible at the employee entrance of the secondary employer.

Certified Union

With a certified union, you can only have an unfair labor practice if there is secondary boycotting pursuant to Section 8(b)(4). Because a certified union is not subject to Section 8(b)(7), it can picket and shut a company down completely without committing an unfair labor practice.

Non-Certified Union

It is an unfair labor practice for an non-certified union to engage in secondary strikes and picketing, e.g. causing delivery people not to cross the lines.

Pure Ally Doctrine

Picketing is permissible at a secondary employer under certain circumstances. For example, *NLRB v. Local 459* (1956) involved a labor dispute between Local 459—the certified bargaining agent of Royal Typewriter's mechanics—and other independent companies who were doing Royal's work while the Royal employees were on a primary strike. A charge was filed and the Board ordered Local 459 to "cease and desist" the secondary picketing.

The Board sought enforcement of its order from the Court of Appeals. The Court of Appeals denied enforcement, holding that the independent companies were so allied with Royal that the union's picketing was not prohibited.

Thus, if a secondary is being paid to do the primary's work while the primary's employees are on strike, the union is permitted to picket at the secondary site. However, where the secondary site serves many employers, including the primary, the signs must clarify that the primary employer is the one involved in the labor dispute.

However, if the independent's work is minimal or unrelated to the primary's normal activities, then picketing the independents would be an unfair labor practice.

Ambulatory Situs

In the case of an ambulatory situs, there must be a balance between the right of the employees to picket versus the rights of the secondary's employees. Thus:

1. Picketing must be limited to the time that the dispute is located at the second situs;

2. The primary must be engaged in normal activities at the situs;

3. Picketing must take place reasonably close to the situs; and

4. Picketing must disclose that the dispute is with the primary.

The Court has held that the common situs is wherever primary and secondary employees work together.

Publicity Provision

It is not an unfair labor practice to picket, or distribute publicity—e.g. handbills—for the purpose of truthfully advising the public that (i) a product is produced by an employer with whom the union has a primary dispute; and (ii) the product is being distributed by another employer.

This is so, provided that such picketing or publicity doesn't have the effect of inducing a secondary distributor's employees (i) to refuse to pick up, deliver, transport goods, or (ii) into not performing services at the secondary distributor's establishment. For this reason, such picketing is not permitted at the employee entrance of the secondary employer.

For example, in *NLRB v. Local 760*, the union struck the fruit packers (primary), who sold apples to the Safeway supermarket chain (secondary). A boycott of the apples, including picketing, was conducted outside of the Safeway supermarkets. There was no attempt to interfere with the store employees, the customers, or deliveries. Picketing was peaceful and conducted only during store hours.

An unfair labor practices charge was filed. The Board held that Section 8(b)(4) prohibited picketing in front of secondary establishments. The Board sought enforcement from the Court of Appeals. The Court of Appeals denied enforcement, holding that in order for there to be a ULP, there must be a showing that the union's conduct "threatened, coerced or restrained," causing a negative economic effect on the Safeway stores.

The Supreme Court granted certiorari and affirmed the Court of Appeals decision. It held that the purpose for the statute was not to proscribe all peaceful consumer picketing, but to prevent unions from appealing to the general public to assist in labor disputes.

Thus, a limited public appeal made solely against the product is permissible. The reasoning is that peaceful picketing of a struck product to inform the consumer keeps the union's appeal closely confined to the primary dispute.

A general picket which seeks to boycott the entire store is an unfair labor practice because it causes customers to avoid the business entirely, with the effect of pressuring the chain to extract concessions from the primary. This is blatant secondary boycotting. Nevertheless, publicity intended to advise the public to boycott the store is permissible provided it does not induce a work stoppage by the secondary's employees.

It is well-established, however, that unions are legally permitted to make a noncoercive request to a secondary employer to stop dealing in the goods or services of the primary employer that is the subject of the union's boycott.

LOCKOUTS

When an employer tries to put economic pressure on a union by refusing to permit its employees to work, this is known as a "lockout."

If an employer locks out its employees in order to place pressure on the union to reach a favorable collective bargaining agreement, this is known as an "offensive lockout." Although not illegal per se, if such activity is accompanied by anti-union animus, it may be deemed illegal under Section 8(a)(3) and (1) of the NLRA. The Court held that a violation of Section 8(a)(3) generally requires a showing of (i) discrimination; (ii) a resulting discouragement of union membership; and (iii) proof of the employer's antiunion motive. The Court further held that an offensive lockout may be deemed illegal "if it is so destructive of collective bargaining that the Board need not inquire into employer motivation."

However, there are instances where lockouts have been held to be legal and necessary. For example, a temporary lockout to preserve a multi-employer unit from disintegration is permissible as long as there is no independent evidence to show that it was done to break the union. This is known as a "defensive lockout."

In *NLRB v. Truck Drivers Local 449* (1957), a union represented truckdrivers of 8 linen employers—known as "The Exchange." The parties had a 13-year history of collective bargaining. Sixty days before expiration of the agreements, the union gave notice of its desire for changes to the agreements. Negotiations carried on past the expiration date. The union struck and picketed one of the Exchange employers. Striking one employer at a time is known as a "whipsaw" strike. The seven other members of the Exchange responded by laying off their employees. Negotiations continued and an agreement was finally reached and signed. The strike ended and the laid off drivers were recalled to work.

The union filed a ULP charge with the Board, alleging that the layoff interfered with Section 7 rights by violating Sections 8(1)(1) and (3) of the NLRA. A complaint was issued and the hearing examiner found the seven Exchange members guilty of an unfair labor practice. In this case, the Board overruled the hearing examiner, finding that the lockout was a defensive act which was privileged and neither retaliatory nor unlawful. The

Court of Appeals reversed the Board's decision. The United States Supreme Court reversed the Court of Appeals and reinstated the Board's ruling.

The Supreme Court held that the NLRA does not make the lockout unlawful per se, stating that there are references in the Taft-Hartley Act which recognize circumstances when lockouts are legal and necessary. The Court held that the Board correctly balanced the conflict and decided the temporary lockout to preserve multi-employer bargaining was lawful.

REINSTATEMENT RIGHTS

Pursuant to Section 2(3) of the NLRA, strikers retain their employee status. Their right to reinstatement depends on whether the strike is a (i) ULP strike; or a (ii) economic strike.

ULP Strike

A ULP strike is one which is initiated in whole or in part in response to an employer's unfair labor practices. In a ULP strike:

1. Employees must be reinstated even if the employer must discharge permanent replacement workers.

2. Employees need not be reinstated if they are guilty of misconduct, subject to a Board determination.

3. Employees remain eligible to vote.

Economic Strike

An economic strike is one which is neither caused or prolonged by an employer's unfair labor practices. In an economic strike:

1. The employer is free to hire permanent replacements and doesn't have to reinstate a striker if his place has been filled during the strike.

2. If the employee is guilty of misconduct, an employer is under no duty to rehire, and the employee cannot vote.

3. Although employees may lose their right to reinstatement, they are eligible to vote in a representative election held within 12 months of commencement of the strike.

4. Strikers are placed on a preferential hiring list according to seniority.

An economic strike can turn into a ULP strike depending on the acts of the employer. For example, if an employer refuses to bargain, this would constitute a ULP violation. In that case, reinstatement would be required.

CHAPTER 8:
THE FEDERAL LABOR RELATIONS AUTHORITY

IN GENERAL

The Federal Labor Relations Authority (FLRA) was established by the Civil Service Reform Act of 1978 (the "Act"). The FLRA establishes policies for Federal sector labor-management relations. It also resolves disputes under, and ensures compliance with Title VII of the Act.

Selected Provisions of the Civil Service Reform Act are set forth at Appendix 14.

The FLRA consists of three independent agencies including the Authority, the Office of the General Counsel and the Federal Service Impasses Panel. The FLRA also supports the Foreign Service Labor Relations Board which was established by the Foreign Service Act of 1980.

THE AUTHORITY

The Authority is a quasi-judicial body with three full-time Members. Members are appointed by the President with the advice and consent of the Senate and serve for five-year terms. The Chairman of the Authority is also appointed by the President. The Authority adjudicates disputes arising under the Act, which includes deciding cases regarding collective bargaining agreement proposals; appeals concerning unfair labor practices and representation petitions; and exceptions to grievance arbitration awards. The Authority also assists Federal agencies and unions in understanding their rights and responsibilities under the Act.

THE OFFICE OF THE GENERAL COUNSEL

The Office of the General Counsel (OGC) is the FLRA's independent investigator and prosecutor. The General Counsel is appointed by the President with the advice and consent of the Senate for a five-year term. The General Counsel is responsible for the management of the OGC, including the management of the FLRA's seven regional offices. The General Counsel is also responsible for processing petitions in representation cases filed with the FLRA. The OGC resolves representation matters by conducting elections and making appropriate unit determinations.

A sample petition in a representation case is set forth at Appendix 15.

The General Counsel also handles unfair labor practice (ULP) allegations. The regional offices investigate, settle, and determine whether to dismiss or prosecute ULP charges. The General Counsel also decides appeals of a Regional Director's decision not to issue a ULP complaint.

THE FEDERAL IMPASSES PANEL

The Federal Service Impasses Panel consists of seven Presidential appointees who serve on a part-time basis, including the Chairman. The Panel resolves impasses between Federal agencies and unions representing Federal employees arising from negotiations over conditions of employment. If bargaining between the parties, followed by mediation assistance, proves unsuccessful, the Panel has the authority to recommend procedures and to take whatever action it deems necessary to resolve the impasse.

THE FOREIGN SERVICE LABOR RELATIONS BOARD

The Foreign Service Labor Relations Board consists of three Members who are appointed by the Chairman of the Authority. The Board was created by the Foreign Service Act of 1980 to administer the labor-management relations program for Foreign Service employees in the U.S. Information Agency, the Agency for International Development, and the Departments of State, Agriculture and Commerce. The Board is supported by the staff of the FLRA. The FLRA Chairman serves as Chairman of the Board and the FLRA General Counsel serves as General Counsel for the Board.

The Foreign Service Impasse Disputes Panel

The Foreign Service Impasse Disputes Panel was also created by the Foreign Service Act of 1980. It consists of five part-time members appointed by the Chairman of the Foreign Service Labor Relations Board. The Panel resolves impasses between Federal agencies and Foreign Service personnel in the U.S. Information Agency, the Agency for International Development and the Departments of State, Agriculture and Commerce over conditions of employment under the Foreign Service Act of 1980. The staff of the Federal Service Impasses Panel supports the Disputes Panel.

TYPES OF AUTHORITY CASES

There are four major categories of cases that come before the Authority Chairman and Members for resolution:

1. Representation Cases;

2. Arbitration Cases;

3. Negotiability Cases; and

4. Unfair Labor Practice Cases

Representation Cases

Applications for review of a Regional Director's Decision and Order in a Representation Case are filed with the Case Control Office. However, neither the filing nor granting of an application for review operates to stay any action ordered by the Regional Director unless the Authority specifically orders a stay. The Authority grants review of a Regional Director's Decision and Order on limited grounds and only when:

1. The Decision and Order raises an issue for which there is an absence of precedent;

2. Established law or policy warrants reconsideration; or

3. There is a genuine issue over which the Regional Director has failed to apply established law, committed a prejudicial procedural error, or committed a clear and prejudicial error concerning a substantial factual matter.

After an application for review is filed, the Authority may deny the application or decide not to undertake review, in which case the Regional Director's decision will stand. If the application for review is granted, the Authority will either resolve the issues based on the existing record or request that the parties to a case provide additional briefs on certain issues. Decisions of the Authority on representation matters are generally not subject to judicial review.

Arbitration Appeals

An agency or union may appeal an arbitrator's decision within 30 days from the date the award is served. Exceptions to arbitration awards are filed with the Case Control Office. Once properly filed, the Authority will review an award to determine whether the award is deficient because:

1. The award is contrary to any law, rule or regulation;

2. The award fails to draw its essence from the collective bargaining agreement;

3. The award is based on a nonfact;

4. The award violates public policy;

5. The arbitrator denied a party a fair hearing;

6. The arbitrator exceeded his or her authority;

7. The award shows bias; or

8. The award is ambiguous, incomplete or contradictory.

The Authority will not consider exceptions to an award relating to actions based on unacceptable performance that are covered under 5 U.S.C. §4303; removals, suspensions for more than 14 days, reductions in grade or pay, or furloughs of 30 days or less that are covered under 5 U.S.C. §7512, and matters similar to those covered under 5 U.S.C. §§4303 and 7512 that arise under other personnel systems. Challenges to these actions may be taken elsewhere.

Authority decisions involving exceptions to arbitration awards are not subject to judicial review, unless the decision involves an unfair labor practice pursuant to section 7118 of the Act.

Negotiability Cases

A union may file a petition for review challenging either an agency head's disapproval of negotiated contract language or an agency's claim that bargaining proposals are contrary to a law, rule or regulation. Petitions for review are filed with the Case Control Office. Shortly after a petition is filed, the Case Control Office contacts the parties in each case and schedules a Post-Petition Conference with representatives of each party. The representatives must be prepared and authorized to discuss such matters as:

1. The meaning of the proposal or provision in dispute;

2. Any disputed factual issues;

3. Negotiability dispute objections and bargaining obligation claims; and

4. Whether the proposal or provision in dispute is also involved in an unfair labor practice charge, grievance or impasse procedure.

Conferences are conducted by Authority staff members. A representative of the Collaboration and Alternative Dispute Resolution Program may also be present to provide information on ADR services and offer settlement assistance.

Following the conclusion of the Conference, a report is served on the parties and position statements are filed. After the position statements have been filed, and the entire record is reviewed, the Authority issues a decision.

Unfair Labor Practice Cases

The Statute sets forth many rights and obligations that are enforced through an unfair labor practice action. If an individual employee, a union, or an agency believes that an unfair labor practice has been committed, that party should contact the appropriate Regional Office for assistance. The Regional Offices are responsible for investigating and processing charges that unfair labor practices have been committed.

A sample charge against an agency is set forth at Appendix 16, and a sample charge against a labor union is set forth at Appendix 17.

In almost all instances, investigations of alleged unlawful conduct, issuance of complaints by Regional Directors and actions taken by an Administrative Law Judge, up to and including preparation of a recommended decision, occur before the Authority's involvement in an unfair labor practice complaint.

On occasion, the Authority becomes involved at earlier stages of an unfair labor practice proceeding. For example, the Authority must approve a formal settlement agreement and a General Counsel request for temporary relief, such as a restraining order.

Exceptions to a recommended decision of an Administrative Law Judge must be filed with the Case Control Office. Any exception that is not specifically argued is deemed waived. When no exceptions to a decision of an Administrative Law Judge are filed, the findings, conclusions and recommendations of the Judge become, without precedential significance, those of the Authority. When exceptions are filed, the Authority, upon review of the recommended findings and conclusions, issues a decision that affirms or reverses, in whole or in part, the decision of the Judge.

In limited circumstances, the Authority will also render a decision in a stipulated unfair labor practice, without a prior decision by an Administrative Law Judge, where the case is transferred directly to the Authority.

If an unfair labor practice has been committed, the Authority will issue an order requiring the party to cease and desist from the unlawful conduct and to take appropriate remedial actions. If there is a finding that no unfair labor practice has been committed, the Authority will dismiss the complaint.

APPENDIX 1:
THE NATIONAL LABOR RELATIONS ACT (NLRA)—Title 29, Chapter 7, Subchapter II, United States Code

SECTION 1. FINDINGS AND POLICIES

[Sec. 151.] The denial by some employers of the right of employees to organize and the refusal by some employers to accept the procedure of collective bargaining lead to strikes and other forms of industrial strife or unrest, which have the intent or the necessary effect of burdening or obstructing commerce by:

(a) impairing the efficiency, safety, or operation of the instrumentalities of commerce;

(b) occurring in the current of commerce;

(c) materially affecting, restraining, or controlling the flow of raw materials or manufactured or processed goods from or into the channels of commerce, or the prices of such materials or goods in commerce; or

(d) causing diminution of employment and wages in such volume as substantially to impair or disrupt the market for goods flowing from or into the channels of commerce.

The inequality of bargaining power between employees who do not possess full freedom of association or actual liberty of contract and employers who are organized in the corporate or other forms of ownership association substantially burdens and affects the flow of commerce, and tends to aggravate recurrent business depressions, by depressing wage rates and the purchasing power of wage earners in industry and by preventing the stabilization of competitive wage rates and working conditions within and between industries.

Experience has proved that protection by law of the right of employees to organize and bargain collectively safeguards commerce from injury, impairment, or interruption, and promotes the flow of commerce by removing certain recognized sources of industrial strife and unrest, by encouraging practices fundamental to the friendly adjustment of industrial disputes arising out of differences as to wages, hours, or other working conditions, and by restoring equality of bargaining power between employers and employees.

Experience has further demonstrated that certain practices by some labor organizations, their officers, and members have the intent or the necessary effect of burdening or obstructing commerce by preventing the free flow of goods in such commerce through strikes and other forms of industrial unrest or through concerted activities which impair the interest of the public in the free flow of such commerce. The elimination of such practices is a necessary condition to the assurance of the rights herein guaranteed.

It is declared to be the policy of the United States to eliminate the causes of certain substantial obstructions to the free flow of commerce and to mitigate and eliminate these obstructions when they have occurred by encouraging the practice and procedure of collective bargaining and by protecting the exercise by workers of full freedom of association, self-organization, and designation of representatives of their own choosing, for the purpose of negotiating the terms and conditions of their employment or other mutual aid or protection.

SECTION 2. DEFINITIONS

[Sec. 152.] When used in this Act [subchapter]—

(1) The term "person" includes one or more individuals, labor organizations, partnerships, associations, corporations, legal representatives, trustees, trustees in cases under title 11 of the United States Code [under title 11], or receivers.

(2) The term "employer" includes any person acting as an agent of an employer, directly or indirectly, but shall not include the United States or any wholly owned Government corporation, or any Federal Reserve Bank, or any State or political subdivision thereof, or any person subject to the Railway Labor Act [45 U.S.C. Sec. 151 et seq.], as amended from time to time, or any labor organization (other than when acting as an employer), or anyone acting in the capacity of officer or agent of such labor organization.

[Pub. L. 93-360, Sec. 1(a), July 26, 1974, 88 Stat. 395, deleted the phrase "or any corporation or association operating a hospital, if no part of the net earnings inures to the benefit of any private shareholder or individual" from the definition of "employer."]

(3) The term "employee" shall include any employee, and shall not be limited to the employees of a particular employer, unless the Act [this subchapter] explicitly states otherwise, and shall include any individual whose work has ceased as a consequence of, or in connection with, any current labor dispute or because of any unfair labor practice, and who has not obtained any other regular and substantially equivalent employment, but shall not include any individual employed as an agricultural laborer, or in the domestic service of any family or person at his home, or any individual employed by his parent or spouse, or any individual having the status of an independent contractor, or any individual employed as a supervisor, or any individual employed by an employer subject to the Railway Labor Act [45 U.S.C. Sec. 151 et seq.], as amended from time to time, or by any other person who is not an employer as herein defined.

(4) The term "representatives" includes any individual or labor organization.

(5) The term "labor organization" means any organization of any kind, or any agency or employee representation committee or plan, in which employees participate and which exists for the purpose, in whole or in part, of dealing with employers concerning grievances, labor disputes, wages, rates of pay, hours of employment, or conditions of work.

(6) The term "commerce" means trade, traffic, commerce, transportation, or communication among the several States, or between the District of Columbia or any Territory of the United States and any State or other Territory, or between any foreign country and any State, Territory, or the District of Columbia, or within the District of Columbia or any Territory, or between points in the same State but through any other State or any Territory or the District of Columbia or any foreign country.

(7) The term "affecting commerce" means in commerce, or burdening or obstructing commerce or the free flow of commerce, or having led or tending to lead to a labor dispute burdening or obstructing commerce or the free flow of commerce.

(8) The term "unfair labor practice" means any unfair labor practice listed in section 8 [section 158 of this title].

(9) The term "labor dispute" includes any controversy concerning terms, tenure, or conditions of employment, or concerning the association or representation of persons in negotiating, fixing, maintaining, changing, or seeking to arrange terms or conditions of employment, regardless of whether the disputants stand in the proximate relation of employer and employee.

(10) The term "National Labor Relations Board" means the National Labor Relations Board provided for in section 3 of this Act [section 153 of this title].

(11) The term "supervisor" means any individual having authority, in the interest of the employer, to hire, transfer, suspend, lay off, recall, promote, discharge, assign, reward, or discipline other employees, or responsibly to direct them, or to adjust their grievances, or effectively to recommend such action, if in connection with the foregoing the exercise of such authority is not of a merely routine or clerical nature, but requires the use of independent judgment.

(12) The term "professional employee" means—

(a) any employee engaged in work (i) predominantly intellectual and varied in character as opposed to routine mental, manual, mechanical, or physical work; (ii) involving the consistent exercise of discretion and judgment in its performance; (iii) of such a character that the output produced or the result accomplished cannot be standardized in relation to a given period of time; (iv) requiring knowledge of an advanced type in a field of science or learning customarily acquired by a prolonged course of specialized intellectual instruction and study in an institution of higher learning or a hospital, as distinguished from a general academic education or from an apprenticeship or from training in the performance of routine mental, manual, or physical processes; or

(b) any employee, who (i) has completed the courses of specialized intellectual instruction and study described in clause (iv) of paragraph (a), and (ii) is performing related work under the supervision of a professional person to qualify himself to become a professional employee as defined in paragraph (a).

(13) In determining whether any person is acting as an "agent" of another person so as to make such other person responsible for his acts, the question of whether the specific acts performed were actually authorized or subsequently ratified shall not be controlling.

(14) The term "health care institution" shall include any hospital, convalescent hospital, health maintenance organization, health clinic, nursing home, extended care facility, or other institution devoted to the care of sick, infirm, or aged person.

[Pub. L. 93-360, Sec. 1(b), July 26, 1974, 88 Stat. 395, added par. (14).]

SECTION 3. THE NATIONAL LABOR RELATIONS BOARD

[Sec. 153.] (a) [Creation, composition, appointment, and tenure; Chairman; removal of members] The National Labor Relations Board (hereinafter called the "Board") created by this Act [subchapter] prior to its amendment by the Labor Management Relations Act, 1947 [29 U.S.C. Sec. 141 et seq.], is continued as an agency of the United States, except that the Board shall consist of five instead of three members, appointed by the President by and with the advice and consent of the Senate. Of the two additional members so provided for, one shall be appointed for a term of five years and the other for a term of two years. Their successors, and the successors of the other members, shall be appointed for terms of five years each, excepting that any individual chosen to fill a vacancy shall be appointed only for the unexpired term of the member whom he shall succeed. The President shall designate one member to serve as Chairman of the Board. Any member of the Board may be removed by the President, upon notice and hearing, for neglect of duty or malfeasance in office, but for no other cause.

(b) [Delegation of powers to members and regional directors; review and stay of actions of regional directors; quorum; seal] The Board is authorized to delegate to any group of three or more members any or all of the powers which it may itself exercise. The Board is also authorized to delegate to its regional directors its powers under section 9 [section 159 of this title] to determine the unit appropriate for the purpose of collective bargaining, to investigate and provide for hearings, and determine whether a question of representation exists, and to direct an election or take a secret ballot under subsection (c) or (e) of section 9 [section 159 of this title] and certify the results thereof, except that upon the filling of a request therefor with the Board by any interested person, the Board may review any action of a regional director delegated to him under this paragraph, but such a review shall not, unless specifically ordered by the Board, operate as a stay of any action taken by the regional director. A vacancy in the Board shall not impair the right of the remaining members to exercise all of the powers of the Board, and three members of the Board shall, at all times, constitute a quorum of the Board, except that two members shall constitute a quorum of any group designated pursuant to the first sentence hereof. The Board shall have an official seal which shall be judicially noticed.

(c) [Annual reports to Congress and the President] The Board shall at the close of each fiscal year make a report in writing to Congress and to the President summarizing significant case activities and operations for that fiscal year.

(d) [General Counsel; appointment and tenure; powers and duties; vacancy] There shall be a General Counsel of the Board who shall be appointed by the President, by and with the advice and consent of the Senate, for a term of four years. The General Counsel of the Board shall exercise general supervision over all attorneys employed by the Board (other than administrative law judges and legal assistants to Board members) and over the officers and employees in the regional offices. He shall have final authority, on behalf of the Board, in respect of the investigation of charges and issuance of complaints under section 10 [section 160 of this title], and in respect of the prosecution of such complaints before the Board, and shall have such other duties as the Board may prescribe or as may be provided by law. In case of vacancy in the office of the General Counsel the President is authorized to designate the officer or employee who shall act as General Counsel during such vacancy, but no person or persons so designated shall so act:

(1) for more than forty days when the Congress is in session unless a nomination to fill such vacancy shall have been submitted to the Senate, or

(2) after the adjournment sine die of the session of the Senate in which such nomination was submitted.

[The title "administrative law judge" was adopted in 5 U.S.C. Sec. 3105.]

SECTION 4. ELIGIBILITY FOR REAPPOINTMENT

[Sec. 154. Eligibility for reappointment; officers and employees; payment of expenses]

(a) Each member of the Board and the General Counsel of the Board shall be eligible for reappointment, and shall not engage in any other business, vocation, or employment. The Board shall appoint an executive secretary, and such attorneys, examiners, and regional directors, and such other employees as it may from time to time find necessary for the proper performance of its duties. The Board may not employ any attorneys for the purpose of reviewing transcripts of hearings or preparing drafts of opinions except that any attorney employed for assignment as a legal assistant to any Board member may for such Board member review such transcripts and prepare such drafts. No administrative law judge's report shall be reviewed, either before or after its publication, by any person other than a member of the Board or his legal assistant, and no administrative law judge shall advise or consult with the Board with respect to exceptions taken to his findings, rulings, or recommendations. The Board may establish or utilize such regional, local, or other agencies, and utilize such voluntary and uncompensated services, as may from time to time be needed. Attorneys appointed under this section may, at the direction of the Board, appear for and represent the Board in any case in court. Nothing in this

Act [subchapter] shall be construed to authorize the Board to appoint individuals for the purpose of conciliation or mediation, or for economic analysis.

[The title "administrative law judge" was adopted in 5 U.S.C. Sec. 3105.]

(b) All of the expenses of the Board, including all necessary traveling and subsistence expenses outside the District of Columbia incurred by the members or employees of the Board under its orders, shall be allowed and paid on the presentation of itemized vouchers therefor approved by the Board or by any individual it designates for that purpose.

SECTION 5. PRINCIPAL OFFICE

[Sec. 155. Principal office, conducting inquiries throughout country; participation in decisions or inquiries conducted by member] The principal office of the Board shall be in the District of Columbia, but it may meet and exercise any or all of its powers at any other place. The Board may, by one or more of its members or by such agents or agencies as it may designate, prosecute any inquiry necessary to its functions in any part of the United States. A member who participates in such an inquiry shall not be disqualified from subsequently participating in a decision of the Board in the same case.

SECTION 6. RULES AND REGULATIONS

[Sec. 156.] The Board shall have authority from time to time to make, amend, and rescind, in the manner prescribed by the Administrative Procedure Act [by subchapter II of chapter 5 of title 5], such rules and regulations as may be necessary to carry out the provisions of this Act [subchapter].

SECTION 7. RIGHTS OF EMPLOYEES

[Sec. 157.] Employees shall have the right to self-organization, to form, join, or assist labor organizations, to bargain collectively through representatives of their own choosing, and to engage in other concerted activities for the purpose of collective bargaining or other mutual aid or protection, and shall also have the right to refrain from any or all such activities except to the extent that such right may be affected by an agreement requiring membership in a labor organization as a condition of employment as authorized in section 8(a)(3) [section 158(a)(3) of this title].

SECTION 8. UNFAIR LABOR PRACTICES

[Sec. 158.] (a) [Unfair labor practices by employer] It shall be an unfair labor practice for an employer—

(1) to interfere with, restrain, or coerce employees in the exercise of the rights guaranteed in section 7 [section 157 of this title];

(2) to dominate or interfere with the formation or administration of any labor organization or contribute financial or other support to it: Provided, That subject to rules and regulations made and published by the Board pursuant to section 6 [section 156 of this title], an employer shall not be prohibited from permitting employees to confer with him during working hours without loss of time or pay;

(3) by discrimination in regard to hire or tenure of employment or any term or condition of employment to encourage or discourage membership in any labor organization: Provided, That nothing in this Act [subchapter], or in any other statute of the United States, shall preclude an employer from making an agreement with a labor organization (not established, maintained, or assisted by any action defined in section 8(a) of this Act [in this subsection] as an unfair labor practice) to require as a condition of employment membership therein on or after the thirtieth day following the beginning of such employment or the effective date of such agreement, whichever is the later, (i) if such labor organization is the representative of the employees as provided in section 9(a) [section 159(a) of this title], in the appropriate collective-bargaining unit covered by such agreement when made, and (ii) unless following an election held as provided in section 9(e) [section 159(e) of this title] within one year preceding the effective date of such agreement, the Board shall have certified that at least a majority of the employees eligible to vote in such election have voted to rescind the authority of such labor organization to make such an agreement: Provided further, That no employer shall justify any discrimination against an employee for nonmembership in a labor organization:

(A) if he has reasonable grounds for believing that such membership was not available to the employee on the same terms and conditions generally applicable to other members, or

(B) if he has reasonable grounds for believing that membership was denied or terminated for reasons other than the failure of the employee to tender the periodic dues and the initiation fees uniformly required as a condition of acquiring or retaining membership;

(4) to discharge or otherwise discriminate against an employee because he has filed charges or given testimony under this Act [subchapter];

(5) to refuse to bargain collectively with the representatives of his employees, subject to the provisions of section 9(a) [section 159(a) of this title].

(b) [Unfair labor practices by labor organization] It shall be an unfair labor practice for a labor organization or its agents—

(1) to restrain or coerce—

(A) employees in the exercise of the rights guaranteed in section 7 [section 157 of this title]: Provided, That this paragraph shall not impair the right of a labor organization to prescribe its own rules with respect to the acquisition or retention of membership therein; or

(B) an employer in the selection of his representatives for the purposes of collective bargaining or the adjustment of grievances;

(2) to cause or attempt to cause an employer to discriminate against an employee in violation of subsection (a)(3) [of subsection (a)(3) of this section] or to discriminate against an employee with respect to whom membership in such organization has been denied or terminated on some ground other than his failure to tender the periodic dues and the initiation fees uniformly required as a condition of acquiring or retaining membership;

(3) to refuse to bargain collectively with an employer, provided it is the representative of his employees subject to the provisions of section 9(a) [section 159(a) of this title];

(4)(i) to engage in, or to induce or encourage any individual employed by any person engaged in commerce or in an industry affecting commerce to engage in, a strike or a refusal in the course of his employment to use, manufacture, process, transport, or otherwise handle or work on any goods, articles, materials, or commodities or to perform any services; or (ii) to threaten, coerce, or restrain any person engaged in commerce or in an industry affecting commerce, where in either case an object thereof is—

(A) forcing or requiring any employer or self-employed person to join any labor or employer organization or to enter into any agreement which is prohibited by section 8(e) [subsection (e) of this section];

(B) forcing or requiring any person to cease using, selling, handling, transporting, or otherwise dealing in the products of any other producer, processor, or manufacturer, or to cease doing business with any other person, or forcing or requiring any other employer to recognize or bargain with a labor organization as the representative of his employees unless such labor organization has been certified as the representative of such employees under the provisions of section 9 [section 159 of this title]: Provided, That nothing contained in this clause (B) shall be construed to make unlawful, where not otherwise unlawful, any primary strike or primary picketing;

(C) forcing or requiring any employer to recognize or bargain with a particular labor organization as the representative of his employees if another labor organization has been certified as the representative of such employees under the provisions of section 9 [section 159 of this title];

(D) forcing or requiring any employer to assign particular work to employees in a particular labor organization or in a particular trade, craft, or class rather than to employees in another labor organization or in another trade, craft, or class, unless such employer is failing to conform to an order or certification of the Board determining the bargaining representative for employees performing such work: Provided, That nothing contained in this subsection (b) [this subsection] shall be construed to make unlawful a refusal by any person to enter upon the premises of any employer (other than his own employer), if the employees of such employer are engaged in a strike ratified or approved by a representative of such employees whom such employer is required to recognize under this Act [subchapter]: Provided further, That for the purposes of this paragraph (4) only, nothing contained in such paragraph shall be construed to prohibit publicity, other than picketing, for the purpose of truthfully advising the public, including consumers and members of a labor organization, that a product or products are produced by an employer with whom the labor organization has a primary dispute and are distributed by another employer, as long as such publicity does not have an effect of inducing any individual employed by any person other than the primary employer in the course of his employment to refuse to pick up, deliver, or transport any goods, or not to perform any services, at the establishment of the employer engaged in such distribution;

(5) to require of employees covered by an agreement authorized under subsection (a)(3) [of this section] the payment, as a condition precedent to becoming a member of such organization, of a fee in an amount which the Board finds excessive or discriminatory under all the circum-

stances. In making such a finding, the Board shall consider, among other relevant factors, the practices and customs of labor organizations in the particular industry, and the wages currently paid to the employees affected;

(6) to cause or attempt to cause an employer to pay or deliver or agree to pay or deliver any money or other thing of value, in the nature of an exaction, for services which are not performed or not to be performed; and

(7) to picket or cause to be picketed, or threaten to picket or cause to be picketed, any employer where an object thereof is forcing or requiring an employer to recognize or bargain with a labor organization as the representative of his employees, or forcing or requiring the employees of an employer to accept or select such labor organization as their collective-bargaining representative, unless such labor organization is currently certified as the representative of such employees:

(A) where the employer has lawfully recognized in accordance with this Act [subchapter] any other labor organization and a question concerning representation may not appropriately be raised under section 9(c) of this Act [section 159(c) of this title],

(B) where within the preceding twelve months a valid election under section 9(c) of this Act [section 159(c) of this title] has been conducted, or

(C) where such picketing has been conducted without a petition under section 9(c) [section 159(c) of this title] being filed within a reasonable period of time not to exceed thirty days from the commencement of such picketing: Provided, That when such a petition has been filed the Board shall forthwith, without regard to the provisions of section 9(c)(1) [section 159(c)(1) of this title] or the absence of a showing of a substantial interest on the part of the labor organization, direct an election in such unit as the Board finds to be appropriate and shall certify the results thereof: Provided further, That nothing in this subparagraph (C) shall be construed to prohibit any picketing or other publicity for the purpose of truthfully advising the public (including consumers) that an employer does not employ members of, or have a contract with, a labor organization, unless an effect of such picketing is to induce any individual employed by any other person in the course of his employment, not to pick up, deliver or transport any goods or not to perform any services. Nothing in this paragraph (7) shall be construed to permit any act which would otherwise be an unfair labor practice under this section 8(b) [this subsection].

(c) [Expression of views without threat of reprisal or force or promise of benefit] The expressing of any views, argument, or opinion, or the dissemination thereof, whether in written, printed, graphic, or visual form, shall not constitute or be evidence of an unfair labor practice under any of the provisions of this Act [subchapter], if such expression contains no threat of reprisal or force or promise of benefit.

(d) [Obligation to bargain collectively] For the purposes of this section, to bargain collectively is the performance of the mutual obligation of the employer and the representative of the employees to meet at reasonable times and confer in good faith with respect to wages, hours, and other terms and conditions of employment, or the negotiation of an agreement or any question arising thereunder, and the execution of a written contract incorporating any agreement reached if requested by either party, but such obligation does not compel either party to agree to a proposal or require the making of a concession: Provided, That where there is in effect a collective-bargaining contract covering employees in an industry affecting commerce, the duty to bargain collectively shall also mean that no party to such contract shall terminate or modify such contract, unless the party desiring such termination or modification—

(1) serves a written notice upon the other party to the contract of the proposed termination or modification sixty days prior to the expiration date thereof, or in the event such contract contains no expiration date, sixty days prior to the time it is proposed to make such termination or modification;

(2) offers to meet and confer with the other party for the purpose of negotiating a new contract or a contract containing the proposed modifications;

(3) notifies the Federal Mediation and Conciliation Service within thirty days after such notice of the existence of a dispute, and simultaneously therewith notifies any State or Territorial agency established to mediate and conciliate disputes within the State or Territory where the dispute occurred, provided no agreement has been reached by that time; and

(4) continues in full force and effect, without resorting to strike or lockout, all the terms and conditions of the existing contract for a period of sixty days after such notice is given or until the expiration date of such contract, whichever occurs later: The duties imposed upon employers, employees, and labor organizations by paragraphs (2), (3), and (4) [paragraphs (2) to (4) of this subsection] shall become inapplicable upon an intervening certification of the Board, under which the labor organization or individual, which is a party to the contract, has been superseded as or ceased to be the representative of the employees sub-

ect to the provisions of section 9(a) [section 159(a) of this title], and the duties so imposed shall not be construed as requiring either party to discuss or agree to any modification of the terms and conditions contained in a contract for a fixed period, if such modification is to become effective before such terms and conditions can be reopened under the provisions of the contract. Any employee who engages in a strike within any notice period specified in this subsection, or who engages in any strike within the appropriate period specified in subsection (g) of this section, shall lose his status as an employee of the employer engaged in the particular labor dispute, for the purposes of sections 8, 9, and 10 of this Act [sections 158, 159, and 160 of this title], but such loss of status for such employee shall terminate if and when he is reemployed by such employer. Whenever the collective bargaining involves employees of a health care institution, the provisions of this section 8(d) [this subsection] shall be modified as follows:

(A) The notice of section 8(d)(1) [paragraph (1) of this subsection] shall be ninety days; the notice of section 8(d)(3) [paragraph (3) of this subsection] shall be sixty days; and the contract period of section 8(d)(4) [paragraph (4) of this subsection] shall be ninety days.

(B) Where the bargaining is for an initial agreement following certification or recognition, at least thirty days' notice of the existence of a dispute shall be given by the labor organization to the agencies set forth in section 8(d)(3) [in paragraph (3) of this subsection].

(C) After notice is given to the Federal Mediation and Conciliation Service under either clause (A) or (B) of this sentence, the Service shall promptly communicate with the parties and use its best efforts, by mediation and conciliation, to bring them to agreement. The parties shall participate fully and promptly in such meetings as may be undertaken by the Service for the purpose of aiding in a settlement of the dispute.

[Pub. L. 93-360, July 26, 1974, 88 Stat. 395, amended the last sentence of Sec. 8(d) by striking the words "the sixty-day" and inserting the words "any notice" and by inserting before the words "shall lose" the phrase "or who engages in any strike within the appropriate period specified in subsection (g) of this section." It also amended the end of paragraph Sec. 8(d) by adding a new sentence "Whenever the collective bargaining . . . aiding in a settlement of the dispute."]

(e) [Enforceability of contract or agreement to boycott any other employer; exception] It shall be an unfair labor practice for any labor organization and any employer to enter into any contract or agreement, express or implied, whereby such employer ceases or refrains or agrees to cease or refrain from handling, using, selling, transporting, or otherwise dealing in any of the products of any other employer, or cease doing business with any other person, and any contract or agreement entered into heretofore or hereafter containing such an agreement shall be to such extent unenforceable and void: Provided, That nothing in this subsection (e) [this subsection] shall apply to an agreement between a labor organization and an employer in the construction industry relating to the contracting or subcontracting of work to be done at the site of the construction, alteration, painting, or repair of a building, structure, or other work: Provided further, That for the purposes of this subsection (e) and section 8(b)(4)(B) [this subsection and subsection (b)(4)(B) of this section] the terms "any employer," "any person engaged in commerce or an industry affecting commerce," and "any person" when used in relation to the terms "any other producer, processor, or manufacturer," "any other employer," or "any other person" shall not include persons in the relation of a jobber, manufacturer, contractor, or subcontractor working on the goods or premises of the jobber or manufacturer or performing parts of an integrated process of production in the apparel and clothing industry: Provided further, That nothing in this Act [subchapter] shall prohibit the enforcement of any agreement which is within the foregoing exception.

(f) [Agreements covering employees in the building and construction industry] It shall not be an unfair labor practice under subsections (a) and (b) of this section for an employer engaged primarily in the building and construction industry to make an agreement covering employees engaged (or who, upon their employment, will be engaged) in the building and construction industry with a labor organization of which building and construction employees are members (not established, maintained, or assisted by any action defined in section 8(a) of this Act [subsection (a) of this section] as an unfair labor practice) because (1) the majority status of such labor organization has not been established under the provisions of section 9 of this Act [section 159 of this title] prior to the making of such agreement, or (2) such agreement requires as a condition of employment, membership in such labor organization after the seventh day following the beginning of such employment or the effective date of the agreement, whichever is later, or (3) such agreement requires the employer to notify such labor organization of opportunities for employment with such employer, or gives such labor organization an opportunity to refer qualified applicants for such employment, or (4) such agreement specifies minimum training or experience qualifications for employment or provides for priority in opportunities for employment based upon length of service with such employer, in the industry or in the particular geographical area: Provided, That nothing in this subsection shall set aside the final proviso to section 8(a)(3) of this Act [subsection (a)(3) of this section]: Provided further, That any agreement which would be invalid, but for clause (1) of this subsection, shall not be a bar to a petition filed pursuant to section 9(c) or 9(e) [section 159(c) or 159(e) of this title].

(g) [Notification of intention to strike or picket at any health care institution] A labor organization before engaging in any strike, picketing, or other concerted refusal to work at any health care institution shall, not less than ten days prior to such action, notify the institution in writing and the Federal Mediation and Conciliation Service of that intention, except that in the case of bargaining for an initial agreement following certification or recognition the notice required by this subsection shall not be given until the expiration of the period specified in clause (B) of the last sentence of section 8(d) of this Act [subsection (d) of this section]. The notice shall state the date and time that such action will commence. The notice, once given, may be extended by the written agreement of both parties.

[Pub. L. 93-360, July 26, 1974, 88 Stat. 396, added subsec. (g).]

SECTION 9. REPRESENTATIVES AND ELECTIONS

[Sec. 159.] (a) [Exclusive representatives; employees' adjustment of grievances directly with employer] Representatives designated or selected for the purposes of collective bargaining by the majority of the employees in a unit appropriate for such purposes, shall be the exclusive representatives of all the employees in such unit for the purposes of collective bargaining in respect to rates of pay, wages, hours of employment, or other conditions of employment: Provided, That any individual employee or a group of employees shall have the right at any time to present grievances to their employer and to have such grievances adjusted, without the intervention of the bargaining representative, as long as the adjustment is not inconsistent with the terms of a collective-bargaining contract or agreement then in effect: Provided further, That the bargaining representative has been given opportunity to be present at such adjustment.

(b) [Determination of bargaining unit by Board] The Board shall decide in each case whether, in order to assure to employees the fullest freedom in exercising the rights guaranteed by this Act [subchapter], the unit appropriate for the purposes of collective bargaining shall be the employer unit, craft unit, plant unit, or subdivision thereof: Provided, That the Board shall not (1) decide that any unit is appropriate for such purposes if such unit includes both professional employees and employees who are not professional employees unless a majority of such professional employees vote for inclusion in such unit; or (2) decide that any craft unit is inappropriate for such purposes on the ground that a different unit has been established by a prior Board determination, unless a majority of the employees in the proposed craft unit votes against separate representation or (3) decide that any unit is appropriate for such purposes if it includes, together with other employees, any individual employed as a guard to enforce against employees and other persons rules to protect property of the employer or to protect the safety of persons on the employer's premises; but no labor organization shall be certified as the representative of employees in a bargaining unit of guards if such organization admits to membership, or is affiliated directly or indirectly with an organization which admits to membership, employees other than guards.

(c) [Hearings on questions affecting commerce; rules and regulations]

(1) Whenever a petition shall have been filed, in accordance with such regulations as may be prescribed by the Board—

(A) by an employee or group of employees or any individual or labor organization acting in their behalf alleging that a substantial number of employees (i) wish to be represented for collective bargaining and that their employer declines to recognize their representative as the representative defined in section 9(a) [subsection (a) of this section], or (ii) assert that the individual or labor organization, which has been certified or is being currently recognized by their employer as the bargaining representative, is no longer a representative as defined in section 9(a) [subsection (a) of this section]; or

(B) by an employer, alleging that one or more individuals or labor organizations have presented to him a claim to be recognized as the representative defined in section 9(a) [subsection (a) of this section]; the Board shall investigate such petition and if it has reasonable cause to believe that a question of representation affecting commerce exists shall provide for an appropriate hearing upon due notice. Such hearing may be conducted by an officer or employee of the regional office, who shall not make any recommendations with respect thereto. If the Board finds upon the record of such hearing that such a question of representation exists, it shall direct an election by secret ballot and shall certify the results thereof.

(2) In determining whether or not a question of representation affecting commerce exists, the same regulations and rules of decision shall apply irrespective of the identity of the persons filing the petition or the kind of relief sought and in no case shall the Board deny a labor organization a place on the ballot by reason of an order with respect to such labor organization or its predecessor not issued in conformity with section 10(c) [section 160(c) of this title].

(3) No election shall be directed in any bargaining unit or any subdivision within which, in the preceding twelve-month period, a valid election shall have been held. Employees engaged in an economic strike who are not entitled to reinstatement shall be eligible to vote under

such regulations as the Board shall find are consistent with the purposes and provisions of this Act [subchapter] in any election conducted within twelve months after the commencement of the strike. In any election where none of the choices on the ballot receives a majority, a runoff shall be conducted, the ballot providing for a selection between the two choices receiving the largest and second largest number of valid votes cast in the election.

(4) Nothing in this section shall be construed to prohibit the waiving of hearings by stipulation for the purpose of a consent election in conformity with regulations and rules of decision of the Board.

(5) In determining whether a unit is appropriate for the purposes specified in subsection (b) [of this section] the extent to which the employees have organized shall not be controlling.

(d) [Petition for enforcement or review; transcript] Whenever an order of the Board made pursuant to section 10(c) [section 160(c) of this title] is based in whole or in part upon facts certified following an investigation pursuant to subsection (c) of this section and there is a petition for the enforcement or review of such order, such certification and the record of such investigation shall be included in the transcript of the entire record required to be filed under section 10(e) or 10(f) [subsection (e) or (f) of section 160 of this title], and thereupon the decree of the court enforcing, modifying, or setting aside in whole or in part the order of the Board shall be made and entered upon the pleadings, testimony, and proceedings set forth in such transcript.

(e) [Secret ballot; limitation of elections]

(1) Upon the filing with the Board, by 30 per centum or more of the employees in a bargaining unit covered by an agreement between their employer and labor organization made pursuant to section 8(a)(3) [section 158(a)(3) of this title], of a petition alleging they desire that such authorization be rescinded, the Board shall take a secret ballot of the employees in such unit and certify the results thereof to such labor organization and to the employer.

(2) No election shall be conducted pursuant to this subsection in any bargaining unit or any subdivision within which, in the preceding twelve-month period, a valid election shall have been held.

SECTION 10. PREVENTION OF UNFAIR LABOR PRACTICES

[Sec. 160.] (a) [Powers of Board generally] The Board is empowered, as hereinafter provided, to prevent any person from engaging in any unfair labor practice (listed in section 8 [section 158 of this title]) affecting commerce. This power shall not be affected by any other means of adjustment or prevention that has been or may be established by agreement, law, or otherwise: Provided, That the Board is empowered by agreement with any agency of any State or Territory to cede to such agency jurisdiction over any cases in any industry (other than mining, manufacturing, communications, and transportation except where predominately local in character) even though such cases may involve labor disputes affecting commerce, unless the provision of the State or Territorial statute applicable to the determination of such cases by such agency is inconsistent with the corresponding provision of this Act [subchapter] or has received a construction inconsistent therewith.

(b) [Complaint and notice of hearing; six-month limitation; answer; court rules of evidence inapplicable] Whenever it is charged that any person has engaged in or is engaging in any such unfair labor practice, the Board, or any agent or agency designated by the Board for such purposes, shall have power to issue and cause to be served upon such person a complaint stating the charges in that respect, and containing a notice of hearing before the Board or a member thereof, or before a designated agent or agency, at a place therein fixed, not less than five days after the serving of said complaint: Provided, That no complaint shall issue based upon any unfair labor practice occurring more than six months prior to the filing of the charge with the Board and the service of a copy thereof upon the person against whom such charge is made, unless the person aggrieved thereby was prevented from filing such charge by reason of service in the armed forces, in which event the six-month period shall be computed from the day of his discharge. Any such complaint may be amended by the member, agent, or agency conducting the hearing or the Board in its discretion at any time prior to the issuance of an order based thereon. The person so complained of shall have the right to file an answer to the original or amended complaint and to appear in person or otherwise and give testimony at the place and time fixed in the complaint. In the discretion of the member, agent, or agency conducting the hearing or the Board, any other person may be allowed to intervene in the said proceeding and to present testimony. Any such proceeding shall, so far as practicable, be conducted in accordance with the rules of evidence applicable in the district courts of the United States under the rules of civil procedure for the district courts of the United States, adopted by the Supreme Court of the United States pursuant to section 2072 of title 28, United States Code [section 2072 of title 28].

(c) [Reduction of testimony to writing; findings and orders of Board] The testimony taken by such member, agent, or agency, or the Board shall be reduced to writing and filed with the Board. Thereafter, in its discretion, the Board upon notice may take further testimony or hear argument. If upon the preponderance of the testimony taken the Board shall be of the opinion that any person named in the complaint has engaged in or is engaging in any such unfair labor practice, then the Board shall state its findings of fact and shall issue and cause to be served on such person an order requiring such person to cease and desist from such unfair labor practice, and to take such affirmative action including reinstatement of employees with or without backpay, as will effectuate the policies of this Act [subchapter]: Provided, That where an order directs reinstatement of an employee, backpay may be required of the employer or labor organization, as the case may be, responsible for the discrimination suffered by him: And provided further, That in determining whether a complaint shall issue alleging a violation of section 8(a)(1) or section 8(a)(2) [subsection (a)(1) or (a)(2) of section 158 of this title], and in deciding such cases, the same regulations and rules of decision shall apply irrespective of whether or not the labor organization affected is affiliated with a labor organization national or international in scope. Such order may further require such person to make reports from time to time showing the extent to which it has complied with the order. If upon the preponderance of the testimony taken the Board shall not be of the opinion that the person named in the complaint has engaged in or is engaging in any such unfair labor practice, then the Board shall state its findings of fact and shall issue an order dismissing the said complaint. No order of the Board shall require the reinstatement of any individual as an employee who has been suspended or discharged, or the payment to him of any backpay, if such individual was suspended or discharged for cause. In case the evidence is presented before a member of the Board, or before an administrative law judge or judges thereof, such member, or such judge or judges, as the case may be, shall issue and cause to be served on the parties to the proceeding a proposed report, together with a recommended order, which shall be filed with the Board, and if no exceptions are filed within twenty days after service thereof upon such parties, or within such further period as the Board may authorize, such recommended order shall become the order of the Board and become affective as therein prescribed.

[The title "administrative law judge" was adopted in 5 U.S.C. Sec. 3105.]

(d) [Modification of findings or orders prior to filing record in court] Until the record in a case shall have been filed in a court, as hereinafter provided, the Board may at any time, upon reasonable notice and in such manner as it shall deem proper, modify or set aside, in whole or in part, any finding or order made or issued by it.

(e) [Petition to court for enforcement of order; proceedings; review of judgment] The Board shall have power to petition any court of appeals of the United States, or if all the courts of appeals to which application may be made are in vacation, any district court of the United States, within any circuit or district, respectively, wherein the unfair labor practice in question occurred or wherein such person resides or transacts business, for the enforcement of such order and for appropriate temporary relief or restraining order, and shall file in the court the record in the proceeding, as provided in section 2112 of title 28, United States Code [section 2112 of title 28]. Upon the filing of such petition, the court shall cause notice thereof to be served upon such person, and thereupon shall have jurisdiction of the proceeding and of the question determined therein, and shall have power to grant such temporary relief or restraining order as it deems just and proper, and to make and enter a decree enforcing, modifying and enforcing as so modified, or setting aside in whole or in part the order of the Board. No objection that has not been urged before the Board, its member, agent, or agency, shall be considered by the court, unless the failure or neglect to urge such objection shall be excused because of extraordinary circumstances. The findings of the Board with respect to questions of fact if supported by substantial evidence on the record considered as a whole shall be conclusive. If either party shall apply to the court for leave to adduce additional evidence and shall show to the satisfaction of the court that such additional evidence is material and that there were reasonable grounds for the failure to adduce such evidence in the hearing before the Board, its member, agent, or agency, the court may order such additional evidence to be taken before the Board, its member, agent, or agency, and to be made a part of the record. The Board may modify its findings as to the facts, or make new findings, by reason of additional evidence so taken and filed, and it shall file such modified or new findings, which findings with respect to question of fact if supported by substantial evidence on the record considered as a whole shall be conclusive, and shall file its recommendations, if any, for the modification or setting aside of its original order. Upon the filing of the record with it the jurisdiction of the court shall be exclusive and its judgment and decree shall be final, except that the same shall be subject to review by the appropriate United States court of appeals if application was made to the district court as hereinabove provided, and by the Supreme Court of the United States upon writ of certiorari or certification as provided in section 1254 of title 28.

(f) [Review of final order of Board on petition to court] Any person aggrieved by a final order of the Board granting or denying in whole or in part the relief sought may obtain a review of such order in any United States court of appeals in the circuit wherein the unfair labor practice in question was alleged to have been engaged in or wherein such person resides or transacts business, or in the United States Court of Appeals for the District of Columbia, by filing in such court a written petition praying that the order of the Board be modified or set aside. A copy of such petition shall be forthwith transmitted by the clerk of the court to the Board, and thereupon the aggrieved party shall file in the court the record in the proceeding, certified by the Board, as provided in section 2112 of title 28,

United States Code [section 2112 of title 28]. Upon the filing of such petition, the court shall proceed in the same manner as in the case of an application by the Board under subsection (e) of this section, and shall have the same jurisdiction to grant to the Board such temporary relief or restraining order as it deems just and proper, and in like manner to make and enter a decree enforcing, modifying and enforcing as so modified, or setting aside in whole or in part the order of the Board; the findings of the Board with respect to questions of fact if supported by substantial evidence on the record considered as a whole shall in like manner be conclusive.

(g) [Institution of court proceedings as stay of Board's order] The commencement of proceedings under subsection (e) or (f) of this section shall not, unless specifically ordered by the court, operate as a stay of the Board's order.

(h) [Jurisdiction of courts unaffected by limitations prescribed in chapter 6 of this title] When granting appropriate temporary relief or a restraining order, or making and entering a decree enforcing, modifying and enforcing as so modified, or setting aside in whole or in part an order of the Board, as provided in this section, the jurisdiction of courts sitting in equity shall not be limited by sections 101 to 115 of title 29, United States Code [chapter 6 of this title] [known as the "Norris-LaGuardia Act"].

(i) Repealed.

(j) [Injunctions] The Board shall have power, upon issuance of a complaint as provided in subsection (b) [of this section] charging that any person has engaged in or is engaging in an unfair labor practice, to petition any United States district court, within any district wherein the unfair labor practice in question is alleged to have occurred or wherein such person resides or transacts business, for appropriate temporary relief or restraining order. Upon the filing of any such petition the court shall cause notice thereof to be served upon such person, and thereupon shall have jurisdiction to grant to the Board such temporary relief or restraining order as it deems just and proper.

(k) [Hearings on jurisdictional strikes] Whenever it is charged that any person has engaged in an unfair labor practice within the meaning of paragraph (4)(D) of section 8(b) [section 158(b) of this title], the Board is empowered and directed to hear and determine the dispute out of which such unfair labor practice shall have arisen, unless, within ten days after notice that such charge has been filed, the parties to such dispute submit to the Board satisfactory evidence that they have adjusted, or agreed upon methods for the voluntary adjustment of, the dispute. Upon compliance by the parties to the dispute with the decision of the Board or upon such voluntary adjustment of the dispute, such charge shall be dismissed.

(l) [Boycotts and strikes to force recognition of uncertified labor organizations; injunctions; notice; service of process] Whenever it is charged that any person has engaged in an unfair labor practice within the meaning of paragraph (4)(A), (B), or (C) of section 8(b) [section 158(b) of this title], or section 8(e) [section 158(e) of this title] or section 8(b)(7) [section 158(b)(7) of this title], the preliminary investigation of such charge shall be made forthwith and given priority over all other cases except cases of like character in the office where it is filed or to which it is referred. If, after such investigation, the officer or regional attorney to whom the matter may be referred has reasonable cause to believe such charge is true and that a complaint should issue, he shall, on behalf of the Board, petition any United States district court within any district where the unfair labor practice in question has occurred, is alleged to have occurred, or wherein such person resides or transacts business, for appropriate injunctive relief pending the final adjudication of the Board with respect to such matter. Upon the filing of any such petition the district court shall have jurisdiction to grant such injunctive relief or temporary restraining order as it deems just and proper, notwithstanding any other provision of law: Provided further, That no temporary restraining order shall be issued without notice unless a petition alleges that substantial and irreparable injury to the charging party will be unavoidable and such temporary restraining order shall be effective for no longer than five days and will become void at the expiration of such period: Provided further, That such officer or regional attorney shall not apply for any restraining order under section 8(b)(7) [section 158(b)(7) of this title] if a charge against the employer under section 8(a)(2) [section 158(a)(2) of this title] has been filed and after the preliminary investigation, he has reasonable cause to believe that such charge is true and that a complaint should issue. Upon filing of any such petition the courts shall cause notice thereof to be served upon any person involved in the charge and such person, including the charging party, shall be given an opportunity to appear by counsel and present any relevant testimony: Provided further, That for the purposes of this subsection district courts shall be deemed to have jurisdiction of a labor organization (1) in the district in which such organization maintains its principal office, or (2) in any district in which its duly authorized officers or agents are engaged in promoting or protecting the interests of employee members. The service of legal process upon such officer or agent shall constitute service upon the labor organization and make such organization a party to the suit. In situations where such relief is appropriate the procedure specified herein shall apply to charges with respect to section 8(b)(4)(D) [section 158(b)(4)(D) of this title].

(m) [Priority of cases] Whenever it is charged that any person has engaged in an unfair labor practice within the meaning of subsection (a)(3) or (b)(2) of section 8 [section 158 of this title], such charge shall be given priority over all other cases except cases of like character in the office where it is filed or to which it is referred and cases given priority under subsection (l) [of this section].

SECTION 11. INVESTIGATORY POWERS

[Sec. 161.] For the purpose of all hearings and investigations, which, in the opinion of the Board, are necessary and proper for the exercise of the powers vested in it by section 9 and section 10 [sections 159 and 160 of this title]—

(1) [Documentary evidence; summoning witnesses and taking testimony] The Board, or its duly authorized agents or agencies, shall at all reasonable times have access to, for the purpose of examination, and the right to copy any evidence of any person being investigated or proceeded against that relates to any matter under investigation or in question. The Board, or any member thereof, shall upon application of any party to such proceedings, forthwith issue to such party subpoenas requiring the attendance and testimony of witnesses or the production of any evidence in such proceeding or investigation requested in such application. Within five days after the service of a subpoena on any person requiring the production of any evidence in his possession or under his control, such person may petition the Board to revoke, and the Board shall revoke, such subpoena if in its opinion the evidence whose production is required does not relate to any matter under investigation, or any matter in question in such proceedings, or if in its opinion such subpoena does not describe with sufficient particularity the evidence whose production is required. Any member of the Board, or any agent or agency designated by the Board for such purposes, may administer oaths and affirmations, examine witnesses, and receive evidence. Such attendance of witnesses and the production of such evidence may be required from any place in the United States or any Territory or possession thereof, at any designated place of hearing.

(2) [Court aid in compelling production of evidence and attendance of witnesses] In case on contumacy or refusal to obey a subpoena issued to any person, any United States district court or the United States courts of any Territory or possession, within the jurisdiction of which the inquiry is carried on or within the jurisdiction of which said person guilty of contumacy or refusal to obey is found or resides or transacts business, upon application by the Board shall have jurisdiction to issue to such person an order requiring such person to appear before the Board, its member, agent, or agency, there to produce evidence if so ordered, or there to give testimony touching the matter under investiga-

tion or in question; and any failure to obey such order of the court may be punished by said court as a contempt thereof.

(3) Repealed.

[Immunity of witnesses. See 18 U.S.C. Sec. 6001 et seq.]

(4) [Process, service, and return; fees of witnesses] Complaints, orders and other process and papers of the Board, its member, agent, or agency, may be served either personally or by registered or certified mail or by telegraph or by leaving a copy thereof at the principal office or place of business of the person required to be served. The verified return by the individual so serving the same setting forth the manner of such service shall be proof of the same, and the return post office receipt or telegraph receipt therefor when registered or certified and mailed or when telegraphed as aforesaid shall be proof of service of the same. Witnesses summoned before the Board, its member, agent, or agency, shall be paid the same fees and mileage that are paid witnesses in the courts of the United States, and witnesses whose depositions are taken and the persons taking the same shall severally be entitled to the same fees as are paid for like services in the courts of the United States.

(5) [Process, where served] All process of any court to which application may be made under this Act [subchapter] may be served in the judicial district wherein the defendant or other person required to be served resides or may be found.

(6) [Information and assistance from departments] The several departments and agencies of the Government, when directed by the President, shall furnish the Board, upon its request, all records, papers, and information in their possession relating to any matter before the Board.

SECTION 12. OFFENSES AND PENALTIES

[Sec. 162.] Any person who shall willfully resist, prevent, impede, or interfere with any member of the Board or any of its agents or agencies in the performance of duties pursuant to this Act [subchapter] shall be punished by a fine of not more than $5,000 or by imprisonment for not more than one year, or both.

SECTION 13. LIMITATIONS

[Sec. 163. Right to strike preserved] Nothing in this Act [subchapter], except as specifically provided for herein, shall be construed so as either to interfere with or impede or diminish in any way the right to strike or to affect the limitations or qualifications on that right.

SECTION 14. CONSTRUCTION OF PROVISIONS

[Sec. 164.] (a) [Supervisors as union members] Nothing herein shall prohibit any individual employed as a supervisor from becoming or remaining a member of a labor organization, but no employer subject to this Act [subchapter] shall be compelled to deem individuals defined herein as supervisors as employees for the purpose of any law, either national or local, relating to collective bargaining.

(b) [Agreements requiring union membership in violation of State law] Nothing in this Act [subchapter] shall be construed as authorizing the execution or application of agreements requiring membership in a labor organization as a condition of employment in any State or Territory in which such execution or application is prohibited by State or Territorial law.

(c) [Power of Board to decline jurisdiction of labor disputes; assertion of jurisdiction by State and Territorial courts]—

(1) The Board, in its discretion, may, by rule of decision or by published rules adopted pursuant to the Administrative Procedure Act [to subchapter II of chapter 5 of title 5], decline to assert jurisdiction over any labor dispute involving any class or category of employers, where, in the opinion of the Board, the effect of such labor dispute on commerce is not sufficiently substantial to warrant the exercise of its jurisdiction: Provided, That the Board shall not decline to assert jurisdiction over any labor dispute over which it would assert jurisdiction under the standards prevailing upon August 1, 1959.

(2) Nothing in this Act [subchapter] shall be deemed to prevent or bar any agency or the courts of any State or Territory (including the Commonwealth of Puerto Rico, Guam, and the Virgin Islands) from assuming and asserting jurisdiction over labor disputes over which the Board declines, pursuant to paragraph (1) of this subsection, to assert jurisdiction.

SECTION 15. OMITTED

[Sec. 165.] [Reference to repealed provisions of bankruptcy statute.]

SECTION 16. SEPARABILITY OF PROVISIONS

[Sec. 166.] If any provision of this Act [subchapter], or the application of such provision to any person or circumstances, shall be held invalid, the remainder of this Act [subchapter], or the application of such provision to persons or circumstances other than those as to which it is held invalid, shall not be affected thereby.

SECTION 17. SHORT TITLE

[Sec. 167.] This Act [subchapter] may be cited as the "National Labor Relations Act."

SECTION 18. OMITTED

[Sec. 168.] [Reference to former sec. 9(f), (g), and (h).]

SECTION 19. INDIVIDUALS WITH RELIGIOUS CONVICTIONS

[Sec. 169.] Any employee who is a member of and adheres to established and traditional tenets or teachings of a bona fide religion, body, or sect which has historically held conscientious objections to joining or financially supporting labor organizations shall not be required to join or financially support any labor organization as a condition of employment; except that such employee may be required in a contract between such employee's employer and a labor organization in lieu of periodic dues and initiation fees, to pay sums equal to such dues and initiation fees to a non-religious, nonlabor organization charitable fund exempt from taxation under section 501(c)(3) of title 26 of the Internal Revenue Code [section 501(c)(3) of title 26], chosen by such employee from a list of at least three such funds, designated in such contract or if the contract fails to designate such funds, then to any such fund chosen by the employee. If such employee who holds conscientious objections pursuant to this section requests the labor organization to use the grievance-arbitration procedure on the employee's behalf, the labor organization is authorized to charge the employee for the reasonable cost of using such procedure.

[Sec. added, Pub. L. 93-360, July 26, 1974, 88 Stat. 397, and amended, Pub. L. 96-593, Dec. 24, 1980, 94 Stat. 3452.]

APPENDIX 2:
THE LABOR MANAGEMENT RELATIONS ACT (LMRA)—Title 29, Chapter 7, United States Code

[Sec. 141.] (a) This Act [chapter] may be cited as the "Labor Management Relations Act, 1947. "[Also known as the "Taft-Hartley Act."]

(b) Industrial strife which interferes with the normal flow of commerce and with the full production of articles and commodities for commerce, can be avoided or substantially minimized if employers, employees, and labor organizations each recognize under law one another's legitimate rights in their relations with each other, and above all recognize under law that neither party has any right in its relations with any other to engage in acts or practices which jeopardize the public health, safety, or interest.

It is the purpose and policy of this Act [chapter], in order to promote the full flow of commerce, to prescribe the legitimate rights of both employees and employers in their relations affecting commerce, to provide orderly and peaceful procedures for preventing the interference by either with the legitimate rights of the other, to protect the rights of individual employees in their relations with labor organizations whose activities affect commerce, to define and proscribe practices on the part of labor and management which affect commerce and are inimical to the general welfare, and to protect the rights of the public in connection with labor disputes affecting commerce.

Sec. 201. [Sec. 171. Declaration of purpose and policy] It is the policy of the United States that—

(a) sound and stable industrial peace and the advancement of the general welfare, health, and safety of the Nation and of the best interest of employers and employees can most satisfactorily be secured by the settlement of issues between employers and employees through the processes of conference and collective bargaining between employers and the representatives of their employees;

(b) the settlement of issues between employers and employees through collective bargaining may by advanced by making available full and adequate governmental facilities for conciliation, mediation, and voluntary arbitration to aid and encourage employers and the representatives of their employees to reach and maintain agreements concerning rates of pay, hours, and working conditions, and to make all reasonable efforts to settle their differences by mutual agreement reached through conferences and collective bargaining or by such methods as may be provided for in any applicable agreement for the settlement of disputes; and

(c) certain controversies which arise between parties to collective-bargaining agreements may be avoided or minimized by making available full and adequate governmental facilities for furnishing assistance to employers and the representatives of their employees in formulating for inclusion within such agreements provision for adequate notice of any proposed changes in the terms of such agreements, for the final adjustment of grievances or questions regarding the application or interpretation of such agreements, and other provisions designed to prevent the subsequent arising of such controversies.

Sec. 202. [Sec. 172. Federal Mediation and Conciliation Service]

(a) [Creation; appointment of Director] There is created an independent agency to be known as the Federal Mediation and Conciliation Service (herein referred to as the "Service, "except that for sixty days after June 23, 1947, such term shall refer to the Conciliation Service of the Department of Labor). The Service shall be under the direction of a Federal Mediation and Conciliation Director (hereinafter referred to as the "Director"), who shall be appointed by the President by and with the advice and consent of the Senate. The Director shall not engage in any other business, vocation, or employment.

(b) [Appointment of officers and employees; expenditures for supplies, facilities, and services] The Director is authorized, subject to the civil service laws, to appoint such clerical and other personnel as may be necessary for the execution of the functions of the Service, and shall fix their compensation in accordance with sections 5101 to 5115 and sections 5331 to 5338 of title 5, United States Code [chapter 51 and subchapter III of chapter 53 of title 5], and may, without regard to the provisions of the civil service laws, appoint such conciliators and mediators as may be necessary to carry out the functions of the Service. The Director is authorized to make such expenditures for supplies, facilities, and services as he deems necessary. Such expenditures shall be allowed and paid upon presentation of itemized vouchers therefor approved by the Director or by any employee designated by him for that purpose.

(c) [Principal and regional offices; delegation of authority by Director; annual report to Congress] The principal office of the Service shall be in the District of Columbia, but the Director may establish regional offices convenient to localities in which labor controversies are likely to arise. The Director may by order, subject to revocation at any time, delegate any authority and discretion conferred upon him by this Act [chapter] to any regional director, or other officer or employee of the Service. The Director may establish suitable procedures for cooperation with State and local mediation agencies. The Director shall make an annual report in writing to Congress at the end of the fiscal year.

(d) [Transfer of all mediation and conciliation services to Service; effective date; pending proceedings unaffected] All mediation and conciliation functions of the Secretary of Labor or the United States Conciliation Service under section 51 [repealed] of title 29, United States Code [this title], and all functions of the United States Conciliation Service under any other law are transferred to the Federal Mediation and Conciliation Service, together with the personnel and records of the United States Conciliation Service. Such transfer shall take effect upon the sixtieth day after June 23, 1947. Such transfer shall not affect any proceedings pending before the United States Conciliation Service or any certification, order, rule, or regulation theretofore made by it or by the Secretary of Labor. The Director and the Service shall not be subject in any way to the jurisdiction or authority of the Secretary of Labor or any official or division of the Department of Labor.

Sec. 203. [Sec. 173. Functions of Service]

(a) [Settlement of disputes through conciliation and mediation] It shall be the duty of the Service, in order to prevent or minimize interruptions of the free flow of commerce growing out of labor disputes, to assist parties to labor disputes in industries affecting commerce to settle such disputes through conciliation and mediation.

(b) [Intervention on motion of Service or request of parties; avoidance of mediation of minor disputes] The Service may proffer its services in any labor dispute in any industry affecting commerce, either upon its own motion or upon the request of one or more of the parties to the dispute, whenever in its judgment such dispute threatens to cause a substantial interruption of commerce. The Director and the Service are directed to avoid attempting to mediate disputes which would have only a minor effect on interstate commerce if State or other conciliation services are available to the parties. Whenever the Service does proffer its services in any dispute, it shall be the duty of the Service promptly to put itself in communication with the parties and to use its best efforts, by mediation and conciliation, to bring them to agreement.

(c) [Settlement of disputes by other means upon failure of conciliation] If the Director is not able to bring the parties to agreement by conciliation within a reasonable time, he shall seek to induce the parties voluntarily to seek other means of settling the dispute without resort to strike, lockout, or other coercion, including submission to the employees in the bargaining unit of the employer's last offer of settlement for approval or rejection in a secret ballot. The failure or refusal of either party to agree to any procedure suggested by the Director shall not be deemed a violation of any duty or obligation imposed by this Act [chapter].

(d) [Use of conciliation and mediation services as last resort] Final adjustment by a method agreed upon by the parties is declared to be the desirable method for settlement of grievance disputes arising over the application or interpretation of an existing collective-bargaining agreement. The Service is directed to make its conciliation and mediation services available in the settlement of such grievance disputes only as a last resort and in exceptional cases.

(e) [Encouragement and support of establishment and operation of joint labor management activities conducted by committees] The Service is authorized and directed to encourage and support the establishment and operation of joint labor management activities conducted by plant, area, and industrywide committees designed to improve labor management relationships, job security and organizational effectiveness, in accordance with the provisions of section 205A [section 175a of this title].

[Pub. L. 95-524, Sec. 6(c)(1), Oct. 27, 1978, 92 Stat. 2020, added subsec. (e).]

(f) [Use of alternative means of dispute resolution procedures; assignment of neutrals and arbitrators] The Service may make its services available to Federal agencies to aid in the resolution of disputes under the provisions of subchapter IV of chapter 5 of title 5. Functions performed by the Service may include assisting parties to disputes related to administrative programs, training persons in skills and procedures employed in alternative means of dispute resolution, and furnishing officers and employees of the Service to act as neutrals. Only officers and employees who are qualified in accordance with section 573 of title 5 may be assigned to act as neutrals. The Service shall consult with the Administrative Conference of the United States and other agencies in maintaining rosters of neutrals and arbitrators, and to adopt such procedures and rules as are necessary to carry out the services authorized in this subsection.

[As amended Nov. 15, 1990, Pub. L. 101-552, Sec. 7, 104 Stat. 2746; Aug. 26, 1992, Pub. L. 102-354, Sec. 5(b)(5), 106 Stat. 946.] [It appears that Sec. 173(f) terminated on October 1, 1995, pursuant to a sunset provision. As of the date of this publication, it does not appear that it was reenacted. Persons having an interest in the application of Sec. 173(f) to proceedings commencing after October 1, 1995, should check to see whether the provision was renewed.]

Sec. 204. [Sec. 174. Co-equal obligations of employees, their representatives, and management to minimize labor disputes]

(a) In order to prevent or minimize interruptions of the free flow of commerce growing out of labor disputes, employers and employees and their representatives, in any industry affecting commerce, shall—

(1) exert every reasonable effort to make and maintain agreements concerning rates of pay, hours, and working conditions, including provision for adequate notice of any proposed change in the terms of such agreements;

(2) whenever a dispute arises over the terms or application of a collective-bargaining agreement and a conference is requested by a party or prospective party thereto, arrange promptly for such a conference to be held and endeavor in such conference to settle such dispute expeditiously; and

(3) in case such dispute is not settled by conference, participate fully and promptly in such meetings as may be undertaken by the Service under this Act [chapter] for the purpose of aiding in a settlement of the dispute.

Sec. 205. [Sec. 175. National Labor-Management Panel; creation and composition; appointment, tenure, and compensation; duties]

(a) There is created a National Labor-Management Panel which shall be composed of twelve members appointed by the President, six of whom shall be elected from among persons outstanding in the field of management and six of whom shall be selected from among persons outstanding in the field of labor. Each member shall hold office for a term of three years, except that any member appointed to fill a vacancy occurring prior to the expiration of the term for which his predecessor was appointed shall be appointed for the remainder of such term, and the terms of office of the members first taking office shall expire, as designated by the President at the time of appointment, four at the end of the first year, four at the end of the second year, and four at the end of the third year after the date of appointment. Members of the panel, when serving on business of the panel, shall be paid compensation at the rate of $25 per day, and shall also be entitled to receive an allowance for actual and necessary travel and subsistence expenses while so serving away from their places of residence.

(b) It shall be the duty of the panel, at the request of the Director, to advise in the avoidance of industrial controversies and the manner in which mediation and voluntary adjustment shall be administered, particularly with reference to controversies affecting the general welfare of the country.

Sec. 205A. [Sec. 175a. Assistance to plant, area, and industrywide labor management committees]

(a) [Establishment and operation of plant, area, and industrywide committees]

(1) The Service is authorized and directed to provide assistance in the establishment and operation of plant, area and industrywide labor management committees which—

(A) have been organized jointly by employers and labor organizations representing employees in that plant, area, or industry; and

(B) are established for the purpose of improving labor management relationships, job security, organizational effectiveness, enhancing economic development or involving workers in decisions affecting their jobs including improving communication with respect to subjects of mutual interest and concern.

(2) The Service is authorized and directed to enter into contracts and to make grants, where necessary or appropriate, to fulfill its responsibilities under this section.

(b) [Restrictions on grants, contracts, or other assistance]

(1) No grant may be made, no contract may be entered into and no other assistance may be provided under the provisions of this section to a plant labor management committee unless the employees in that plant are represented by a labor organization and there is in effect at that plant a collective bargaining agreement.

(2) No grant may be made, no contract may be entered into and no other assistance may be provided under the provisions of this section to an area or industrywide labor management committee unless its participants include any labor organizations certified or recognized as the representative of the employees of an employer participating in such committee. Nothing in this clause shall prohibit participation in an area or industrywide committee by an employer whose employees are not represented by a labor organization.

(3) No grant may be made under the provisions of this section to any labor management committee which the Service finds to have as one of its purposes the discouragement of the exercise of rights contained in section 7 of the National Labor Relations Act (29 U.S.C. Sec. 157) [section 157 of this title], or the interference with collective bargaining in any plant, or industry.

(c) [Establishment of office] The Service shall carry out the provisions of this section through an office established for that purpose.

(d) [Authorization of appropriations] There are authorized to be appropriated to carry out the provisions of this section $10,000,000 for the fiscal year 1979, and such sums as may be necessary thereafter.

[Pub. L. 95-524, Sec. 6(c)(2), Oct. 27, 1978, 92 Stat. 2020, added Sec. 205A.]

Sec. 206. [Sec. 176. Appointment of board of inquiry by President; report; contents; filing with Service] Whenever in the opinion of the President of the United States, a threatened or actual strike or lockout affecting an entire industry or a substantial part thereof engaged in trade, commerce, transportation, transmission, or communication among the several States or with foreign nations, or engaged in the production of goods for commerce, will, if permitted to occur or to continue, imperil the national health or safety, he may appoint a board of inquiry to inquire into the issues involved in the dispute and to make a written report to him within such time as he shall prescribe. Such report shall include a statement of the facts with respect to the dispute, including each party's statement of its position but shall not contain any recommendations. The President shall file a copy of such report with the Service and shall make its contents available to the public.

Sec. 207. [Sec. 177. Board of inquiry]

(a) [Composition] A board of inquiry shall be composed of a chairman and such other members as the President shall determine, and shall have power to sit and act in any place within the United States and to conduct such hearings either in public or in private, as it may deem necessary or proper, to ascertain the facts with respect to the causes and circumstances of the dispute.

(b) [Compensation] Members of a board of inquiry shall receive compensation at the rate of $50 for each day actually spent by them in the work of the board, together with necessary travel and subsistence expenses.

(c) [Powers of discovery] For the purpose of any hearing or inquiry conducted by any board appointed under this title [29 U.S.C.S. Sec. Sec. 171-183], the provisions of sections 9 and 10 (relating to the attendance of witnesses and the production of books, papers, and documents) of the Federal Trade Commission Act of September 16 [26], 1914, as amended (U.S.C. [19], title 15, secs. 49 and 50, as amended), are hereby made applicable to the powers and duties of such board. (June 23, 1947, ch 120 Title II, Sec. 61 Stat. 155.)

Sec. 208. [Sec. 178. Injunctions during national emergency]

(a) [Petition to district court by Attorney General on direction of President] Upon receiving a report from a board of inquiry the President may direct the Attorney General to petition any district court of the United States having jurisdiction of the parties to enjoin such strike or lockout or the continuing thereof, and if the court finds that such threatened or actual strike or lockout—

(i) affects an entire industry or a substantial part thereof engaged in trade, commerce, transportation, transmission, or communication among the several States or with foreign nations, or engaged in the production of goods for commerce; and

(ii) if permitted to occur or to continue, will imperil the national health or safety, it shall have jurisdiction to enjoin any such strike or lockout, or the continuing thereof, and to make such other orders as may be appropriate.

(b) [Inapplicability of chapter 6] In any case, the provisions of sections 101 to 115 of title 29, United States Code [chapter 6 of this title] [known as the "Norris-LaGuardia Act"] shall not be applicable.

(c) [Review of orders] The order or orders of the court shall be subject to review by the appropriate circuit court of appeals [court of appeals] and by the Supreme Court upon writ of certiorari or certification as provided in sections 239 and 240 of the Judicial Code, as amended (U.S.C., title 29, secs. 346 and 347). (June 23, 1947, ch 120, Title II Sec. 208, 61 Stat. 155.)

Sec. 209. [Sec. 179. Injunctions during national emergency; adjustment efforts by parties during injunction period]

(a) [Assistance of Service; acceptance of Service's proposed settlement] Whenever a district court has issued an order under section 208 [section 178 of this title] enjoining acts or practices which imperil or threaten to imperil the national health or safety, it shall be the duty of the parties to the labor dispute giving rise to such order to make every effort to adjust and settle their differences, with the assistance of the Service created by this Act [chapter]. Neither party shall be under any duty to accept, in whole or in part, any proposal of settlement made by the Service.

(b) [Reconvening of board of inquiry; report by board; contents; secret ballot of employees by National Labor Relations Board; certification of results to Attorney General] Upon the issuance of such order, the President shall reconvene the board of inquiry which has previously reported with respect to the dispute. At the end of a sixty-day period (unless the dispute has been settled by that time), the board of inquiry shall report to the President the current position of the parties and the efforts which have been made for settlement, and shall include a statement by each party of its position and a statement of the employer's last offer of settlement. The President shall make such report available to the public. The National Labor Relations Board, within the succeeding fifteen days, shall take a secret ballot of the employees of each employer involved in the dispute on the question of whether they wish to accept the final offer of settlement made by their employer, as stated by him, and shall certify the results thereof to the Attorney General within five days thereafter.

Sec. 210. [Sec. 180. Discharge of injunction upon certification of results of election or settlement; report to Congress] Upon the certification of the results of such ballot or upon a settlement being reached, whichever happens sooner, the Attorney General shall move the court to discharge the injunction, which motion shall then be granted, and the injunction discharged. When such motion is granted, the President shall submit to the Congress a full and comprehensive report of the proceedings, including the findings of the board of inquiry and the ballot taken by the National Labor Relations Board, together with such recommendations as he may see fit to make for consideration and appropriate action.

Sec. 211. [Sec. 181.] (a) For the guidance and information of interested representatives of employers, employees, and the general public, the Bureau of Labor Statistics of the Department of Labor shall maintain a file of copies of all available collective-bargaining agreements and other available agreements and actions thereunder settling or adjusting labor disputes. Such file shall be open to inspection under appropriate conditions prescribed by the Secretary of Labor, except that no specific information submitted in confidence shall be disclosed.

(b) The Bureau of Labor Statistics in the Department of Labor is authorized to furnish upon request of the Service, or employers, employees, or their representatives, all available data and factual information which may aid in the settlement of any labor dispute, except that no specific information submitted in confidence shall be disclosed.

Sec. 212. [Sec. 182.] The provisions of this title [subchapter] shall not be applicable with respect to any matter which is subject to the provisions of the Railway Labor Act [45 U.S.C. Sec. 151 et seq.], as amended from time to time.

Sec. 213. [Sec. 183.]

(a) [Establishment of Boards of Inquiry; membership] If, in the opinion of the Director of the Federal Mediation and Conciliation Service, a threatened or actual strike or lockout affecting a health care institution will, if permitted to occur or to continue, substantially interrupt the delivery of health care in the locality concerned, the Director may further assist in the resolution of the impasse by establishing within thirty days after the notice to the Federal Mediation and Conciliation Service under clause (A) of the last sentence of section 8(d) [section 158(d) of this title] (which is required by clause (3) of such section 8(d) [section 158(d) of this title]), or within ten days after the notice under clause (B), an impartial Board of Inquiry to investigate the issues involved in the dispute and to make a written report thereon to the parties within fifteen (15) days after the establishment of such a Board. The written report shall contain the findings of fact together with the Board's recommendations for settling the dispute, with the objective of achieving a prompt, peaceful and just settlement of the dispute. Each such Board shall be composed of such number of individuals as the Director may deem desirable. No member appointed under this section shall have any interest or involvement in the health care institutions or the employee organizations involved in the dispute.

(b) [Compensation of members of Boards of Inquiry]

(1) Members of any board established under this section who are otherwise employed by the Federal Government shall serve without compensation but shall be reimbursed for travel, subsistence, and other necessary expenses incurred by them in carrying out its duties under this section.

(2) Members of any board established under this section who are not subject to paragraph (1) shall receive compensation at a rate prescribed by the Director but not to exceed the daily rate prescribed for GS-18 of the General Schedule under section 5332 of title 5, United States Code [section 5332 of title 5], including travel for each day they are engaged in the performance of their duties under this section and shall be entitled to reimbursement for travel, subsistence, and other necessary expenses incurred by them in carrying out their duties under this section.

(c) [Maintenance of status quo] After the establishment of a board under subsection (a) of this section and for fifteen days after any such board has issued its report, no change in the status quo in effect prior to the expiration of the contract in the case of negotiations for a contract renewal, or in effect prior to the time of the impasse in the case of an initial bargaining negotiation, except by agreement, shall be made by the parties to the controversy.

(d) [Authorization of appropriations] There are authorized to be appropriated such sums as may be necessary to carry out the provisions of this section.

Sec. 301. [Sec. 185.]

(a) [Venue, amount, and citizenship] Suits for violation of contracts between an employer and a labor organization representing employees in an industry affecting commerce as defined in this Act [chapter], or between any such labor organization, may be brought in any district court of the

United States having jurisdiction of the parties, without respect to the amount in controversy or without regard to the citizenship of the parties.

(b) [Responsibility for acts of agent; entity for purposes of suit; enforcement of money judgments] Any labor organization which represents employees in an industry affecting commerce as defined in this Act [chapter] and any employer whose activities affect commerce as defined in this Act [chapter] shall be bound by the acts of its agents. Any such labor organization may sue or be sued as an entity and in behalf of the employees whom it represents in the courts of the United States. Any money judgment against a labor organization in a district court of the United States shall be enforceable only against the organization as an entity and against its assets, and shall not be enforceable against any individual member or his assets.

(c) [Jurisdiction] For the purposes of actions and proceedings by or against labor organizations in the district courts of the United States, district courts shall be deemed to have jurisdiction of a labor organization—

(1) in the district in which such organization maintains its principal offices, or

(2) in any district in which its duly authorized officers or agents are engaged in representing or acting for employee members.

(d) [Service of process] The service of summons, subpoena, or other legal process of any court of the United States upon an officer or agent of a labor organization, in his capacity as such, shall constitute service upon the labor organization.

(e) [Determination of question of agency] For the purposes of this section, in determining whether any person is acting as an "agent "of another person so as to make such other person responsible for his acts, the question of whether the specific acts performed were actually authorized or subsequently ratified shall not be controlling.

Sec. 302. [Sec. 186.]

(a) [Payment or lending, etc., of money by employer or agent to employees, representatives, or labor organizations] It shall be unlawful for any employer or association of employers or any person who acts as a labor relations expert, adviser, or consultant to an employer or who acts in the interest of an employer to pay, lend, or deliver, or agree to pay, lend, or deliver, any money or other thing of value—

(1) to any representative of any of his employees who are employed in an industry affecting commerce; or

(2) to any labor organization, or any officer or employee thereof, which represents, seeks to represent, or would admit to membership, any of the employees of such employer who are employed in an industry affecting commerce;

(3) to any employee or group or committee of employees of such employer employed in an industry affecting commerce in excess of their normal compensation for the purpose of causing such employee or group or committee directly or indirectly to influence any other employees in the exercise of the right to organize and bargain collectively through representatives of their own choosing; or

(4) to any officer or employee of a labor organization engaged in an industry affecting commerce with intent to influence him in respect to any of his actions, decisions, or duties as a representative of employees or as such officer or employee of such labor organization.

(b) [Request, demand, etc., for money or other thing of value]

(1) It shall be unlawful for any person to request, demand, receive, or accept, or agree to receive or accept, any payment, loan, or delivery of any money or other thing of value prohibited by subsection (a) of this section.

(2) It shall be unlawful for any labor organization, or for any person acting as an officer, agent, representative, or employee of such labor organization, to demand or accept from the operator of any motor vehicle (as defined in section 13102 of title 49) employed in the transportation of property in commerce, or the employer of any such operator, any money or other thing of value payable to such organization or to an officer, agent, representative or employee thereof as a fee or charge for the unloading, or in connection with the unloading, of the cargo of such vehicle: Provided, That nothing in this paragraph shall be construed to make unlawful any payment by an employer to any of his employees as compensation for their services as employees.

(c) [Exceptions] The provisions of this section shall not be applicable—

(1) in respect to any money or other thing of value payable by an employer to any of his employees whose established duties include acting openly for such employer in matters of labor relations or personnel administration or to any representative of his employees, or to any officer or employee of a labor organization, who is also an employee or former employee of such employer, as compensation for, or by reason of, his service as an employee of such employer;

(2) with respect to the payment or delivery of any money or other thing of value in satisfaction of a judgment of any court or a decision or

award of an arbitrator or impartial chairman or in compromise, adjustment, settlement, or release of any claim, complaint, grievance, or dispute in the absence of fraud or duress;

(3) with respect to the sale or purchase of an article or commodity at the prevailing market price in the regular course of business;

(4) with respect to money deducted from the wages of employees in payment of membership dues in a labor organization: Provided, That the employer has received from each employee, on whose account such deductions are made, a written assignment which shall not be irrevocable for a period of more than one year, or beyond the termination date of the applicable collective agreement, whichever occurs sooner;

(5) with respect to money or other thing of value paid to a trust fund established by such representative, for the sole and exclusive benefit of the employees of such employer, and their families and dependents (or of such employees, families, and dependents jointly with the employees of other employers making similar payments, and their families and dependents): Provided, That—

(A) such payments are held in trust for the purpose of paying, either from principal or income or both, for the benefit of employees, their families and dependents, for medical or hospital care, pensions on retirement or death of employees, compensation for injuries or illness resulting from occupational activity or insurance to provide any of the foregoing, or unemployment benefits or life insurance, disability and sickness insurance, or accident insurance;

(B) the detailed basis on which such payments are to be made is specified in a written agreement with the employer, and employees and employers are equally represented in the administration of such fund, together with such neutral persons as the representatives of the employers and the representatives of employees may agree upon and in the event the employer and employee groups deadlock on the administration of such fund and there are no neutral persons empowered to break such deadlock, such agreement provides that the two groups shall agree on an impartial umpire to decide such dispute, or in event of their failure to agree within a reasonable length of time, an impartial umpire to decide such dispute shall, on petition of either group, be appointed by the district court of the United States for the district where the trust fund has its principal office, and shall also contain provisions for an annual audit of the trust fund, a statement of the results of which shall be available for inspection by interested persons at the principal office of the trust fund and at such other places as may be designated in such written agreement; and

(C) such payments as are intended to be used for the purpose of providing pensions or annuities for employees are made to a separate trust which provides that the funds held therein cannot be used for any purpose other than paying such pensions or annuities;

(6) with respect to money or other thing of value paid by any employer to a trust fund established by such representative for the purpose of pooled vacation, holiday, severance or similar benefits, or defraying costs of apprenticeship or other training programs: Provided, That the requirements of clause (B) of the proviso to clause (5) of this subsection shall apply to such trust funds;

(7) with respect to money or other thing of value paid by any employer to a pooled or individual trust fund established by such representative for the purpose of—

(A) scholarships for the benefit of employees, their families, and dependents for study at educational institutions,

(B) child care centers for preschool and school age dependents of employees, or

(C) financial assistance for employee housing: Provided, That no labor organization or employer shall be required to bargain on the establishment of any such trust fund, and refusal to do so shall not constitute an unfair labor practice: Provided further, That the requirements of clause (B) of the proviso to clause (5) of this subsection shall apply to such trust funds;

(8) with respect to money or any other thing of value paid by any employer to a trust fund established by such representative for the purpose of defraying the costs of legal services for employees, their families, and dependents for counsel or plan of their choice: Provided, That the requirements of clause (B) of the proviso to clause (5) of this subsection shall apply to such trust funds: Provided further, That no such legal services shall be furnished:

(A) to initiate any proceeding directed (i) against any such employer or its officers or agents except in workman's compensation cases, or (ii) against such labor organization, or its parent or subordinate bodies, or their officers or agents, or (iii) against any other employer or labor organization, or their officers or agents, in any matter arising under subchapter II of this chapter or this chapter; and

(B) in any proceeding where a labor organization would be prohibited from defraying the costs of legal services by the provisions of the Labor-Management Reporting and Disclosure Act of 1959 [29 U.S.C.A. Sec. 401 et seq.]; or (9) with respect to money or other things of value paid by an employer to a plant, area or industrywide labor management committee established for one or more of the purposes set forth in section 5(b) of the Labor Management Cooperation Act of 1978.

[Sec. 302(c)(7) was added by Pub. L. 91-86, Oct. 14, 1969, 83 Stat. 133; Sec. 302(c)(8) by Pub. L. 93-95, Aug. 15, 1973, 87 Stat. 314; Sec. 302(c)(9) by Pub. L. 95-524, Oct. 27, 1978, 92 Stat. 2021; and Sec. 302(c)(7) was amended by Pub. L. 101-273, Apr. 18, 1990, 104 Stat. 138.]

(d) [Penalty for violations]

(1) Any person who participates in a transaction involving a payment, loan, or delivery of money or other thing of value to a labor organization in payment of membership dues or to a joint labor-management trust fund as defined by clause (B) of the proviso to clause (5) of subsection (c) of this section or to a plant, area, or industrywide labor-management committee that is received and used by such labor organization, trust fund, or committee, which transaction does not satisfy all the applicable requirements of subsections (c)(4) through (c)(9) of this section, and willfully and with intent to benefit himself or to benefit other persons he knows are not permitted to receive a payment, loan, money, or other thing of value under subsections (c)(4) through (c)(9) violates this subsection, shall, upon conviction thereof, be guilty of a felony and be subject to a fine of not more than $15,000, or imprisoned for not more than five years, or both; but if the value of the amount of money or thing of value involved in any violation of the provisions of this section does not exceed $1,000, such person shall be guilty of a misdemeanor and be subject to a fine of not more than $10,000, or imprisoned for not more than one year, or both.

(2) Except for violations involving transactions covered by subsection (d)(1) of this section, any person who willfully violates this section shall, upon conviction thereof, be guilty of a felony and be subject to a fine of not more than $15,000, or imprisoned for not more than five years, or both; but if the value of the amount of money or thing of value involved in any violation of the provisions of this section does not exceed $1,000, such person shall be guilty of a misdemeanor and be subject to a fine of not more than $10,000, or imprisoned for not more than one year, or both.

[As amended Oct. 27, 1978, Pub. L. 95-524, Sec. 6(d), 92 Stat. 2021; Oct. 12, 1984, Pub. L. 98-473, Title II, Sec. 801, 98 Stat. 2131; Apr. 18, 1990, Pub. L. 101-273, Sec. 1, 104 Stat. 138.]

(e) [Jurisdiction of courts] The district courts of the United States and the United States courts of the Territories and possessions shall have jurisdiction, for cause shown, and subject to the provisions of rule 65 of the Federal Rules of Civil Procedure [section 381 (repealed) of title 28] (relating to notice to opposite party) to restrain violations of this section, without regard to the provisions of section 7 of title 15 and section 52 of title 29, United States Code [of this title] [known as the "Clayton Act"], and the provisions of sections 101 to 115 of title 29, United States Code [chapter 6 of this title] [known as the "Norris-LaGuardia Act"].

(f) [Effective date of provisions] This section shall not apply to any contract in force on June 23, 1947, until the expiration of such contract, or until July 1, 1948, whichever first occurs.

(g) [Contributions to trust funds] Compliance with the restrictions contained in subsection (c)(5)(B) [of this section] upon contributions to trust funds, otherwise lawful, shall not be applicable to contributions to such trust funds established by collective agreement prior to January 1, 1946, nor shall subsection (c)(5)(A) [of this section] be construed as prohibiting contributions to such trust funds if prior to January 1, 1947, such funds contained provisions for pooled vacation benefits.

Sec. 303. [Sec. 187.]

(a) It shall be unlawful, for the purpose of this section only, in an industry or activity affecting commerce, for any labor organization to engage in any activity or conduct defined as an unfair labor practice in section 8(b)(4) of the National Labor Relations Act [section 158(b)(4) of this title].

(b) Whoever shall be injured in his business or property by reason of any violation of subsection (a) [of this section] may sue therefor in any district court of the United States subject to the limitation and provisions of section 301 hereof [section 185 of this title] without respect to the amount in controversy, or in any other court having jurisdiction of the parties, and shall recover the damages by him sustained and the cost of the suit.

Sec. 304. Repealed. [See sec. 316 of the Federal Election Campaign Act of 1972, 2 U.S.C. Sec. 441b.]

Sec. 305. [Sec. 188.] Strikes by Government employees. Repealed. [See 5 U.S.C. Sec. 7311 and 18 U.S.C. Sec. 1918.]

Secs. 401-407. [Sec. Sec. 191-197.] Omitted.

Sec. 501. [Sec. 142. Definitions] When used in this Act [chapter]—

(1) The term "industry affecting commerce" means any industry or activity in commerce or in which a labor dispute would burden or obstruct commerce or tend to burden or obstruct commerce or the free flow of commerce.

(2) The term "strike" includes any strike or other concerted stoppage of work by employees (including a stoppage by reason of the expiration of a collective-bargaining agreement) and any concerted slowdown or other concerted interruption of operations by employees.

(3) The terms "commerce," "labor disputes," "employer," "employee," "labor organization," "representative," "person," and "supervisor" shall have the same meaning as when used in the National Labor Relations Act as amended by this Act [in subchapter II of this chapter].

Sec. 502. [Sec. 143.] [Abnormally dangerous conditions] Nothing in this Act [chapter] shall be construed to require an individual employee to render labor or service without his consent, nor shall anything in this Act [chapter] be construed to make the quitting of his labor by an individual employee an illegal act; nor shall any court issue any process to compel the performance by an individual employee of such labor or service, without his consent; nor shall the quitting of labor by an employee or employees in good faith because of abnormally dangerous conditions for work at the place of employment of such employee or employees be deemed a strike under this Act [chapter].

Sec. 503. [Sec. 144.] If any provision of this Act [chapter], or the application of such provision to any person or circumstance, shall be held invalid, the remainder of this Act [chapter], or the application of such provision to persons or circumstances other than those as to which it is held invalid, shall not be affected thereby.

APPENDIX 3:
SELECTED PROVISIONS OF THE NLRB
RULES AND REGULATIONS—PART 102

SUBPART B—PROCEDURE UNDER SECTION 10 (A) TO (I) OF THE ACT FOR THE PREVENTION OF UNFAIR LABOR PRACTICES

Charge

Sec. 102.9 Who may file; withdrawal and dismissal.—A charge that any person has engaged in or is engaging in any unfair labor practice affecting commerce may be made by any person. Any such charge may be withdrawn, prior to the hearing, only with the consent of the Regional Director with whom such charge was filed; at the hearing and until the case has been transferred to the Board pursuant to section 102.45, upon motion, with the consent of the administrative law judge designated to conduct the hearing; and after the case has been transferred to the Board pursuant to section 102.45, upon motion, with the consent of the Board. Upon withdrawal of any charge, any complaint based thereon shall be dismissed by the Regional Director issuing the complaint, the administrative law judge designated to conduct the hearing, or the Board.

Sec. 102.10 Where to file.—Except as provided in section 102.33 such charge shall be filed with the Regional Director for the Region in which the alleged unfair labor practice has occurred or is occurring. A charge alleging that an unfair labor practice has occurred or is occuring in two or more Regions may be filed with the Regional Director for any such Regions.

Sec. 102.12 Contents.—Such charge shall contain the following:

(a) The full name and address of the person making the charge.

(b) If the charge is filed by a labor organization, the full name and address of any national or international labor organization of which it is an affiliate or constituent unit.

(c) The full name and address of the person against whom the charge is made (hereinafter referred to as the respondent).

(d) A clear and concise statement of the facts constituting the alleged unfair labor practices affecting commerce.

Complaint

Sec. 102.15 When and by whom issued; contents; service.—After a charge has been filed, if it appears to the Regional Director that formal proceedings in respect thereto should be instituted, he shall issue and cause to be served on all the other parties a formal complaint in the name of the Board stating the unfair labor practices and containing a notice of hearing before an administrative law judge at a place therein fixed and at a time not less than 14 days after the service of the complaint. The complaint shall contain (a) a clear and concise statement of the facts upon which assertion of jurisdiction by the Board is predicated, and (b) a clear and concise description of the acts which are claimed to constitute unfair labor practices, including, where known, the approximate dates and places of such acts and the names of respondent's agents or other representatives by whom committed.

Sec. 102.18 Withdrawal. Any such complaint may be withdrawn before the hearing by the Regional Director on his own motion.

Sec. 102.19 Appeal to the General Counsel from refusal to issue or reissue.—

(a) If, after the charge has been filed, the Regional Director declines to issue a complaint or, having withdrawn a complaint pursuant to section 102.18, refuses to reissue it, he shall so advise the parties in writing, accompanied by a simple statement of the procedural or other grounds for his action...The appeal shall contain a complete statement setting forth the facts and reasons upon which it is based. . .

(b) Oral presentation in Washington, D.C., of the appeal issues may be permitted a party on written request made within 4 days after service of acknowledgement of the filing of an appeal. In the event such request is granted, the other parties shall be notified and afforded, without additional request, a like opportunity at another appropriate time.

(c) The General Counsel may sustain the Regional Director's refusal to issue or reissue a complaint, stating the grounds of his affirmance, or may direct the Regional Director to take further action; the General Counsel's decision shall be served on all the parties. A motion for reconsideration of the decision must be filed within 14 days of service of the decision, except as hereinafter provided, and shall state with particularity the error requiring reconsideration. A motion for reconsideration based upon newly discovered evidence which has become available only since the decision on appeal shall be filed promptly on discovery of such evidence. Motions for reconsideration of a decision previously reconsidered will not be entertained, except in unusual situations where the moving party can establish that new evidence has been discovered which could not have been discovered by diligent inquiry prior to the first reconsideration.

Answer

Sec. 102.20 Answer to complaint; time for filing; contents; allegations not denied deemed admitted.—The respondent shall, within 14 days from the service of the complaint, file an answer thereto. The respondent shall specifically admit, deny, or explain each of the facts alleged in the complaint, unless the respondent is without knowledge, in which case the respondent shall so state, such statement operating as a denial. All allegations in the complaint, if no answer is filed, or any allegation in the complaint not specifically denied or explained in an answer filed, unless the respondent shall state in the answer that he is without knowledge, shall be deemed to be admitted to be true and shall be so found by the Board, unless good cause to the contrary is shown.

Witnesses, Depositions, and Subpoenas

Sec. 102.30 Examination of witnesses; deposition.—Witnesses shall be examined orally under oath, except that for good cause shown after the issuance of a complaint, testimony may be taken by deposition.

Sec. 102.31 Issuance of subpoenas; petitions to revoke subpoenas; right to inspect or copy data.—

(a) Any Member of the Board shall, on the written application of any party, forthwith issue subpoenas requiring the attendance and testimony of witnesses and the production of any evidence, including books, records, correspondence, or documents, in their possession or under their control. Applications for subpoenas, if filed prior to the hearing, shall be filed with the Regional Director. Applications for subpoenas filed during the hearing shall be filed with the administrative law judge. Either the Regional Director or the administrative law judge, as the case may be, shall grant the application on behalf of any Member of the Board. Applications for subpoenas may be made ex parte. The subpoena shall show on its face the name and address of the party at whose request the subpoena was issued.

Hearings

Sec. 102.34 Who shall conduct; to be public unless otherwise ordered.—The hearing for the purpose of taking evidence upon a complaint shall be conducted by an administrative law judge designated by the chief administrative law judge in Washington, D.C., by the deputy chief judge in San Francisco, California, by the associate chief judge in New York, New York, or by the associate chief judge in Atlanta, Georgia, as the case may be, unless the Board or any Member thereof presides. At any time an administrative law judge may be designated to take the place of the administrative law judge previously designated to conduct the hearing. Such hearings shall be public unless otherwise ordered by the Board or the administrative law judge.

Sec. 102.35 Duties and powers of administrative law judges; assignment and powers of settlement judges.—

(a) It shall be the duty of the administrative law judge to inquire fully into the facts as to whether the respondent has engaged in or is engaging in an unfair labor practice affecting commerce as set forth in the complaint or amended complaint. The administrative law judge shall have authority, with respect to cases assigned to him, between the time he is designated and transfer of the case to the Board, subject to the Rules and Regulations of the Board and within its powers:

(1) To administer oaths and affirmations;

(2) To grant applications for subpoenas;

(3) To rule upon petitions to revoke subpoenas;

(4) To rule upon offers of proof and receive relevant evidence;

(5) To take or cause depositions to be taken whenever the ends of justice would be served thereby;

(6) To regulate the course of the hearing and, if appropriate or necessary, to exclude persons or counsel from the hearing for contemptuous conduct and to strike all related testimony of witnesses refusing to answer any proper question;

(7) To hold conferences for the settlement or simplification of the issues by consent of the parties, but not to adjust cases;

(8) To dispose of procedural requests, motions, or similar matters, including motions referred to the administrative law judge by the Regional Director and motions for summary judgment or to amend pleadings; also to dismiss complaints or portions thereof; to order hearings reopened; and upon motion order proceedings consoli-

dated or severed prior to issuance of administrative law judge decisions;

(9) To approve a stipulation voluntarily entered into by all parties to the case which will dispense with a verbatim written transcript of record of the oral testimony adduced at the hearing, and which will also provide for the waiver by the respective parties of their right to file with the Board exceptions to the findings of fact (but not to conclusions of law or recommended orders) which the administrative law judge shall make in his decision;

(10) To make and file decisions, including bench decisions delivered within 72 hours after conclusion of oral argument, in conformity with Public Law 89-554, 5 U.S.C. Sec. 557;

(11) To call, examine, and cross-examine witnesses and to introduce into the record documentary or other evidence;

(12) To request the parties at any time during the hearing to state their respective positions concerning any issue in the case or theory in support thereof;

(13) To take any other action necessary under the foregoing and authorized by the published Rules and Regulations of the Board.

Sec. 102.38 Rights of parties.—Any party shall have the right to appear at such hearing in person, by counsel, or by other representative, to call, examine, and cross-examine witnesses, and to introduce into the record documentary or other evidence, except that the participation of any party shall be limited to the extent permitted by the administrative law judge: And provided further, That documentary evidence shall be submitted in duplicate.

Administrative Law Judge's Decision and Transfer of Case to the Board

Sec. 102.45 Administrative law judge's decision; contents; service; transfer of case to the Board; contents of record in case.—

(a) After hearing for the purpose of taking evidence upon a complaint, the administrative law judge shall prepare a decision. Such decision shall contain findings of fact, conclusions, and the reasons or basis therefor, upon all material issues of fact, law, or discretion presented on the record, and shall contain recommendations as to what disposition of the case should be made, which may include, if it be found that the respondent has engaged in or is engaging in the alleged unfair labor practices, a recommendation for such affirmative action by the respondent as will effectuate the policies of the Act . . .

Procedure Before the Board

Sec. 102.48 Action of Board upon expiration of time to file exceptions to administrative law judge's decision; decisions by the Board; extraordinary postdecisional motions.—

(a) In the event no timely or proper exceptions are filed as herein provided, the findings, conclusions, and recommendations contained in the administrative law judge's decision shall, pursuant to section 10(c) of the Act, automatically become the decision and order of the Board and become its findings, conclusions, and order, and all objections and exceptions thereto shall be deemed waived for all purposes.

(b) Upon the filing of timely and proper exceptions, and any cross-exceptions or answering briefs, as provided in section 102.46, the Board may decide the matter forthwith upon the record, or after oral argument, or may reopen the record and receive further evidence before a Member of the Board or other Board agent or agency, or may make other disposition of the case.

Compliance Proceedings

Sec. 102.52 Compliance with Board order; notification of compliance determination.—After entry of a Board order directing remedial action, or the entry of a court judgment enforcing such order, the Regional Director shall seek compliance from all persons having obligations thereunder. The Regional Director shall make a compliance determination as appropriate and shall notify the parties of the compliance determination. A charging party adversely affected by a monetary, make-whole, reinstatement, or other compliance determination will be provided, on request, with a written statement of the basis for that determination.

Sec. 102.53 Review by the General Counsel of compliance determination; appeal to the Board of the General Counsel's decision.—

(a) The charging party may appeal such determination to the General Counsel in Washington, D.C., within 14 days of the written statement of compliance determination provided as set forth in section 102.52. The appeal shall contain a complete statement setting forth the facts and reasons upon which it is based and shall identify with particularity the error claimed in the Regional Director's determination. The charging party shall serve a copy of the appeal on all other parties and on the Regional Director. The General Counsel may for good cause shown extend the time for filing an appeal.

(b) The General Counsel may affirm or modify the determination of the Regional Director, or may take such other action deemed appropriate, stating the grounds for the decision.

(c) Within 14 days after service of the General Counsel's decision, the charging party may file a request for review of that decision with the Board in Washington, D.C. The request for review shall contain a complete statement of the facts and reasons upon which it is based and shall identify with particularity the error claimed in the General Counsel's decision. A copy of the request for review shall be served on the General Counsel and on the Regional Director.

(d) The Board may affirm or modify the decision of the General Counsel, or make such other disposition of the matter as it deems appropriate. The denial of the request for review will constitute an affirmance of the decision of the General Counsel.

SUBPART C—PROCEDURE UNDER SECTION 9(C) OF THE ACT FOR THE DETERMINATION OF QUESTIONS CONCERNING REPRESENTATION OF EMPLOYEES AND FOR CLARIFICATION OF BARGAINING UNITS AND FOR AMENDMENT OF CERTIFICATIONS UNDER SECTION 9(B) OF THE ACT

Sec. 102.60 Petitions.

(a) Petition for certification or decertification; who may file; where to file; withdrawal.—A petition for investigation of a question concerning representation of employees under paragraphs (1)(A)(i) and (1)(B) of section 9(c) of the Act (hereinafter called a petition for certification) may be filed by an employee or group of employees or any individual or labor organization acting in their behalf or by an employer. A petition under paragraph (1)(A)(ii) of section 9(c) of the Act, alleging that the individual or labor organization which has been certified or is being currently recognized as the bargaining representative is no longer such representative (hereinafter called a petition for decertification), may be filed by any employee or group of employees or any individual or labor organization acting in their behalf . . .

(b) Petition for clarification of bargaining unit or petition for amendment of certification under section 9(b) of the Act; who may file; where to file; withdrawal.—A petition for clarification of an existing bargaining unit or a petition for amendment of certification, in the absence of a question concerning representation, may be filed by a labor organization or by an employer . . .

Sec. 102.61 Contents of petition for certification; contents of petition for decertification; contents of petition for clarification of bargaining unit; contents of petition for amendment of certification.—

(a) A petition for certification, when filed by an employee or group of employees or an individual or labor organization acting in their behalf, shall contain the following:

(1) The name of the employer.

(2) The address of the establishment involved.

(3) The general nature of the employer's business.

(4) A description of the bargaining unit which the petitioner claims to be appropriate.

(5) The names and addresses of any other persons or labor organizations who claim to represent any employees in the alleged appropriate unit and brief descriptions of the contracts, if any, covering the employees in such unit.

(6) The number of employees in the alleged appropriate unit.

(7) A statement that the employer declines to recognize the petitioner as the representative within the meaning of section 9(a) of the Act or that the labor organization is currently recognized but desires certification under the Act.

(8) The name, the affiliation, if any, and the address of the petitioner.

(9) Whether a strike or picketing is in progress at the establishment involved and, if so, the approximate number of employees participating, and the date such strike or picketing commenced.

(10) Any other relevant facts.

(b) A petition for certification, when filed by an employer, shall contain the following:

(1) The name and address of the petitioner.

(2) The general nature of the petitioner's business.

(3) A brief statement setting forth that one or more individuals or labor organizations have presented to the petitioner a claim to be recognized as the exclusive representative of all employees in the unit claimed to be appropriate; a description of such unit; and the number of employees in the unit.

(4) The name or names, the affiliation, if any, and the addresses of the individuals or labor organizations making such claim for recognition.

(5) A statement whether the petitioner has contracts with any labor organization or other representatives of employees and, if so, their expiration dates.

(6) Whether a strike or picketing is in progress at the establishment involved and, if so, the approximate number of employees participating, and the date such strike or picketing commenced.

(7) Any other relevant facts.

(c) A petition for decertification shall contain the following:

(1) The name of the employer.

(2) The address of the establishment and a description of the bargaining unit involved.

(3) The general nature of the employer's business.

(4) The name, the affiliation, if any, and the address of the petitioner.

(5) The name or names of the individuals or labor organizations who have been certified or are being currently recognized by the employer and who claim to represent any employees in the unit involved, and the expiration dates of any contracts covering such employees.

(6) An allegation that the individuals or labor organizations who have been certified or are currently recognized by the employer are no longer the representative in the appropriate unit as defined in section 9(a) of the Act.

(7) The number of employees in the unit.

(8) Whether a strike or picketing is in progress at the establishment involved and, if so, the approximate number of employees participating, and the date such strike or picketing commenced.

(9) Any other relevant facts.

(d) A petition for clarification shall contain the following:

(1) The name of the employer and the name of the recognized or certified bargaining representative.

(2) The address of the establishment involved.

(3) The general nature of the employer's business.

(4) A description of the present bargaining unit and, if the bargaining unit is certified, an identification of the existing certification.

(5) A description of the proposed clarification.

(6) The names and addresses of any other persons or labor organizations who claim to represent any employees affected by the proposed clarifications and brief descriptions of the contracts, if any, covering any such employees.

(7) The number of employees in the present bargaining unit and in the unit as proposed under the clarification.

(8) The job classifications of employees as to whom the issue is raised and the number of employees in each classification.

(9) A statement by petitioner setting forth reasons why petitioner desires clarification of unit.

(10) The name, the affiliation, if any, and the address of the petitioner.

(11) Any other relevant facts.

(e) A petition for amendment of certification shall contain the following:

(1) The name of the employer and the name of the certified union involved.

(2) The address of the establishment involved.

(3) The general nature of the employer's business.

(4) Identification and description of the existing certification.

(5) A statement by petitioner setting forth the details of the desired amendment and reasons therefor.

(6) The names and addresses of any other persons or labor organizations who claim to represent any employees in the unit covered by the certification and brief descriptions of the contracts, if any, covering the employees in such unit.

(7) The name, the affiliation, if any, and the address of the petitioner.

(8) Any other relevant facts.

Sec. 102.62 Consent-election agreements.—

(a) Where a petition has been duly filed, the employer and any individual or labor organizations representing a substantial number of employees involved may, with the approval of the Regional Director, enter into a consent-election agreement leading to a determination by the Regional Director of the facts ascertained after such consent election. Such agreement shall include a description of the appropriate unit, the time and place of holding the election, and the payroll period to be used in determining what employees within the appropriate unit shall be eligible to vote. Such consent election shall be conducted under the direction and supervision of the Regional Director...[T]he rulings and determinations by the Regional Director of the results thereof shall be final, and the Regional Director shall issue to the parties a certification of the results of the election . . .

Sec. 102.64 Conduct of hearing.—

(a) Hearings shall be conducted by a hearing officer and shall be open to the public unless otherwise ordered by the hearing officer. At any time a hearing officer may be substituted for the hearing officer previously presiding. It shall be the duty of the hearing officer to inquire fully into all matters in issue and necessary to obtain a full and complete record upon which the Board or the Regional Director may discharge their duties under section 9(c) of the Act.

Sec. 102.69 Election procedure; tally of ballots; objections; certification by the Regional Director; report on challenged ballots; report on objections; exceptions; action of the Board; hearing.—

(a) Unless otherwise directed by the Board, all elections shall be conducted under the supervision of the Regional Director in whose Region the proceeding is pending. All elections shall be by secret ballot . . .

(b) If no objections are filed within the time set forth above, if the challenged ballots are insufficient in number to affect the results of the election, and if no runoff election is to be held pursuant to section 102.70, the Regional Director shall forthwith issue to the parties a certification of the results of the election, including certifications of representative where appropriate, with the same force and effect as if issued by the Board, and the proceeding will thereupon be closed.

(c)(1) If timely objections are filed to the conduct of the election or to conduct affecting the results of the election, or if the challenged ballots are sufficient in number to affect the results of the election, the Regional Director shall, consistent with the provisions of section 102.69(d), initiate an investigation, as required, of such objections or challenges.

Sec. 102.70 Runoff election.—

(a) The Regional Director shall conduct a runoff election, without further order of the Board, when an election in which the ballot provided for not less than three choices (i.e., at least two representatives and "neither") results in no choice receiving a majority of the valid ballots cast and no objections are filed as provided in section 102.69. Only one runoff election shall be held pursuant to this section.

(b) Employees who were eligible to vote in the election and who are in an eligible category on the date of the runoff election shall be eligible to vote in the runoff election.

(c) The ballot in the runoff election shall provide for a selection between the two choices receiving the largest and second largest number of votes.

Sec. 102.71 Dismissal of petition; refusal to proceed with petition; requests for review by Board of action of the Regional Director.—

(a) If, after a petition has been filed and at any time prior to the close of hearing, it shall appear to the Regional Director that no further proceedings are warranted, the Regional Director may dismiss the petition by administrative action and shall so advise the petitioner in writing, setting forth a simple statement of the procedural or other grounds for the dismissal, with copies to the other parties to the proceeding . . . A request for review from an action of a Regional Director pursuant to this subsection may be granted only upon one or more of the following grounds:

(1) That a substantial question of law or policy is raised because of (i) the absence of, or (ii) a departure from, officially reported Board precedent.

(2) There are compelling reasons for reconsideration of an important Board rule or policy.

(3) The request for review is accompanied by documentary evidence previously submitted to the Regional Director raising serious doubts as to the Regional Director's factual findings, thus indicating that there are factual issues which can best be resolved upon the basis of the record developed at a hearing.

(4) The Regional Director's action is, on its face, arbitrary or capricious.

(5) The petition raises issues which can best be resolved upon the basis of a record developed at a hearing.

(b) Where the Regional Director dismisses a petition or directs that the proceeding on the petition be held in abeyance, and such action is taken because of the pendency of concurrent unresolved charges of unfair labor practices, and the Regional Director, upon request, has so notified the parties in writing, any party may obtain a review of the Regional Director's action by filing a request therefor with the Board in Washington, D.C., in accordance with the provisions of subsection (c) of this section. A review of an action of a Regional Director pursuant to this subsection may be granted only upon one or more of the following grounds:

(1) That a substantial question of law or policy is raised because of (i) the absence of, or (ii) a departure from, officially reported Board precedent.

(2) There are compelling reasons for reconsideration of an important Board rule or policy.

(3) The Regional Director's action is, on its face, arbitrary or capricious.

SUBPART D—PROCEDURE FOR UNFAIR LABOR PRACTICE AND REPRESENTATION CASES UNDER SECTIONS 8(B)(7) AND 9(C) OF THE ACT

Sec. 102.73 Initiation of proceedings.—Whenever it is charged that any person has engaged in an unfair labor practice within the meaning of section 8(b)(7) of the Act, the Regional Director shall investigate such charge, giving it the priority specified in subpart G of these rules.

Sec. 102.74 Complaint and formal proceedings.—If it appears to the Regional Director that the charge has merit, formal proceedings in respect thereto shall be instituted in accordance with the procedures described in sections 102.15 to 102.51, inclusive, insofar as they are applicable, and insofar as they are not inconsistent with the provisions of this subpart. If it appears to the Regional Director that issuance of a complaint is not warranted, he shall decline to issue a complaint, and the provisions of section 102.19, including the provisions for appeal to the General Counsel, shall be applicable unless an election has been directed under sections 102.77 and 102.78, in which event the provisions of section 102.81 shall be applicable.

Sec. 102.76 Petition; who may file; where to file; contents.—When picketing of an employer has been conducted for an object proscribed by section 8(b)(7) of the Act, a petition for the determination of a question concerning representation of the employees of such employer may be filed in accordance with the provisions of sections 102.60 and 102.61, insofar as applicable: Provided, however, That if a charge under section 102.73 has been filed against the labor organization on whose behalf picketing has been conducted, the petition shall not be required to contain a statement that the employer declines to recognize the petitioner as the representative within the meaning of section 9(a) of the Act; or that the labor organization is currently recognized but desires certification under the Act; or that the individuals or labor organizations who have been certified or are currently recognized by the employer are no longer the representative; or, if the petitioner is an employer, that one or more individuals or labor organizations have presented to the petitioner a claim to be recognized as the exclusive representative of the employees in the unit claimed to be appropriate.

Sec. 102.78 Election procedure; method of conducting balloting; postballoting procedure.—If no agreement such as that provided in section 102.79 has been made, the Regional Director shall fix the time and place of the election, eligibility requirements for voting, and other arrangements for the balloting. The method of conducting the balloting and the postballoting procedure shall be governed, insofar as applicable, by the provisions of sections 102.69 and 102.70, except that the labor organization on whose behalf picketing has been conducted may not have its name removed from the ballot without the consent of the Regional Director and except that the Regional Director's rulings on any objections or challenged ballots shall be final unless the Board grants special permission to appeal from the Regional Director's rulings. Any request for such permission shall be filed promptly, in writing, and shall briefly state the grounds relied on. The party requesting review shall immediately serve a copy thereof on each other party. A request for review shall not operate as a stay of the Regional Director's rulings unless so ordered by the Board.

Sec. 102.79 Consent-election agreements.—Where a petition has been duly filed, the parties involved may, subject to the approval of the Regional Director, enter into an agreement governing the method of conducting the election as provided for in section 102.62(a), insofar as applicable.

SUBPART F—PROCEDURE TO HEAR AND DETERMINE DISPUTES UNDER SECTION 10(K) OF THE ACT

Sec. 102.89 Initiation of proceedings.—Whenever it is charged that any person has engaged in an unfair labor practice within the meaning of paragraph (4)(D) of section 8(b) of the Act, the Regional Director of the office in which such charge is filed or to which it is referred shall, as soon as possible after the charge has been filed, serve on the parties a copy of the charge together with a notice of the filing of the charge and shall investigate such charge and if it is deemed appropriate to seek injunctive relief of a district court pursuant to section 10(l) of the Act, he shall give it priority over all other cases in the office except other cases under section 10(l) and cases of like character.

SUBPART G—PROCEDURE IN CASES UNDER SECTION 10(J), (L), AND (M) OF THE ACT

Sec. 102.94 Expeditious processing of section 10(j) cases.—

(a) Whenever temporary relief or a restraining order pursuant to section 10(j) of the Act has been procured by the Board, the complaint which has been the basis for such temporary relief or restraining order shall be heard expeditiously and the case shall be given priority by the Board in its successive steps following the issuance of the complaint (until ultimate enforcement or dismissal by the appropriate circuit court of appeals) over all other cases except cases of like character and cases under section 10(l) and (m) of the Act.

Sec. 102.95 Priority of cases pursuant to section 10(l) and (m) of the Act.—

(a) Whenever a charge is filed alleging the commission of an unfair labor practice within the meaning of paragraph (4)(A), (B), (C), or (7) of section 8(b) of the Act, or section 8(e) of the Act, the Regional Office in which such charge is filed or to which it is referred shall give it priority over all other cases in the office except cases of like character and cases under paragraph (4)(D) of section 8(b) of the Act in which it is deemed appropriate to seek injunctive relief of a district court pursuant to section 10(l) of the Act.

(b) Whenever a charge is filed alleging the commission of an unfair labor practice within the meaning of subsection (a)(3) or (b)(2) of section 8 of the Act, the Regional Office in which such charge is filed or to which it is referred shall give it priority over all other cases in the office except cases of like character and cases under section 10(l) of the Act.

Sec. 102.97 Expeditious processing of section 10(l) and (m) cases in successive stages.—

(a) Any complaint issued pursuant to section 102.95(a) or, in a case in which it is deemed appropriate to seek injunctive relief of a district court pursuant to section 10(l) of the Act, any complaint issued pursuant to section 102.93 or notice of hearing issued pursuant to section 102.90 shall be heard expeditiously and the case shall be given priority in such successive steps following its issuance (until ultimate enforcement or dismissal by the appropriate circuit court of appeals) over all cases except cases of like character.

(b) Any complaint issued pursuant to section 102.95(b) shall be heard expeditiously and the case shall be given priority in its successive steps following its issuance (until ultimate enforcement or dismissal by the appropriate circuit court of appeals) over all cases except cases of like character and cases under section 10(l) of the Act.

SUBPART S—OPEN MEETINGS

Sec. 102.137 Public observation of Board meetings.—Every portion of every meeting of the Board shall be open to public observation, except as provided in section 102.139 of these rules, and Board Members shall not jointly conduct or dispose of Agency business other than in accordance with the provisions of this subpart.

APPENDIX 4:
NATIONAL LABOR RELATIONS BOARD—DIRECTORY OF REGIONAL AND SUBREGIONAL OFFICES

REGION	ADDRESS	TELEPHONE	FAX	REGIONAL DIRECTOR
Region 1	Boston Federal Office Building, 10 Causeway Street, Sixth Floor, Boston, Massachusetts 02222-1072	(617) 565-6700	(617) 565-6725	Rosemary Pye
Region 2	Jacob K. Javits Federal Building, 26 Federal Plaza, Room 3614, New York, New York 10278-0104	(212) 264-0300	(212) 264-2450	Celeste Mattina
Region 3	Federal Building, 111 West Huron Street, Room 901, Buffalo, New York 14202-2387	(716) 551-4931	(716) 551-4972	Sandra Dunbar
Region 4	615 Chestnut Street, One Independence Mall, Seventh Floor, Philadelphia, Pennsylvania 19106-4404	(215) 597-7601	(215) 597-7658	Dorothy L. Moore-Duncan

REGION	ADDRESS	TELEPHONE	FAX	REGIONAL DIRECTOR
Region 5	The Appraisers Store Building, 103 South Gay Street, Eighth Floor, Baltimore, Maryland 21202-4026	(410) 962-2822	(410) 962-2198	Wayne Gold
Region 6	William S. Moorehead Federal Building, 1000 Liberty Avenue, Room 1501, Pittsburgh, Pennsylvania 15222-4173	(412) 395-4400	(412) 395-5986	Gerald Kobell
Region 7	Patrick V. McNamara Federal Building, 477 Michigan Avenue, Room 300, Detroit, Michigan 48226-2569	(313) 226-3200	(313) 226-2090	William C. Schaub, Jr.
Region 8	Anthony J. Celebrezze Federal Building, 1240 East Ninth Street, Room 1695, Cleveland, Ohio 44199-2086	(216) 522-3716	(216) 522-2418	Frederick Calatrello
Region 9	Federal Office Building, 550 Main Street, Room 3003, Cincinnati, Ohio 45202-3721	(513) 684-3686	(513) 684-3946	Richard L. Ahearn
Region 10	Harris Tower, 233 Peachtree St. N.E., Suite 1000, Atlanta, Georgia 30303-1531	(404) 331-2896	(404) 331-2858	Martin M. Arlook

REGION	ADDRESS	TELEPHONE	FAX	REGIONAL DIRECTOR
Region 11	Republic Square, 4035 University Parkway, Suite 200, Winston-Salem, North Carolina 27116-1467	(336) 631-5201	(336) 631-5210	Willie L. Clark, Jr.
Region 12	Enterprise Plaza, 201 E. Kennedy Boulevard, Suite 530, Tampa, Florida 33602-5824	(813) 228-2641	(813) 228-2874	Rochelle Kentov
Region 13	200 West Adams Street, Suite 800, Chicago, Illinois 60606-5208	(312) 353-7570	(312) 886-1341	Elizabeth Kinney
Region 14	1222 Spruce Street, Room 8302, St. Louis, Missouri 63103-2829	(314) 539-7770	(314) 539-7794	Ralph R. Tremain
Region 15	1515 Poydras Street, Room 610, New Orleans, Louisiana 70112-3723	(504) 589-6361	(504) 589-4069	James Paulsen
Region 16	Federal Office Building, 819 Taylor Street, Room 8A24, Fort Worth, Texas 76102-6178	(817) 978-2921	(817) 978-2928	Curtis A. Wells
Region 17	8600 Farley Street, Suite 100, Overland Park, Kansas 66212-4677	(913) 967-3000	(913) 967-3010	F. Rozier Sharp
Region 18	Towle Building, 330 Second Avenue S., Suite 790, Minneapolis, Minnesota 55401-2221	(612) 348-1757	(612) 348-1785	Ronald M. Sharp

REGION	ADDRESS	TELEPHONE	FAX	REGIONAL DIRECTOR
Region 19	Henry M. Jackson Federal Building, 915 Second Avenue, Room 2948, Seattle, Washington 98174-1078	(206) 220-6300	(206) 220-6305	Paul Eggert
Region 20	901 Market Street, Suite 400, San Francisco, California 94103-1735	(415) 356-5130	(415) 356-5156	Robert H. Miller
Region 21	888 South Figueroa Street, Ninth Floor, Los Angeles, California 90017-5449	(213) 894-5200	(213) 894-2778	Victoria E. Aguayo
Region 22	20 Washington Place, 5th Floor, Newark, New Jersey 07102-2570	(973) 645-2100	(973) 645-3852	Gary T. Kendellen
Region 24	La Torre de Plaza, 525 F.D. Roosevelt Ave., Suite 1002, San Juan, Puerto Rico 00918-1002	(787) 766-5347	(787) 766-5478	Marta Figueroa
Region 25	Minton-Capehart Federal Building, 575 North Pennsylvania Street, Room 238, Indianapolis, Indiana 46204-1577	(317) 226-7430	(317) 226-5103	Roberto G. Chavarry
Region 26	Mid-Memphis Tower Building, 1407 Union Avenue, Suite 800, Memphis, Tennessee 38104-3627	(901) 544-0018	(901) 544-0008	Ronald K. Hooks

REGION	ADDRESS	TELEPHONE	FAX	REGIONAL DIRECTOR
Region 27	600 17th Street, 7th Floor, North Tower, Denver, Colorado 80202-5433	(303) 844-3551	(303) 844-6249	B. Allan Benson
Region 28	2600 North Central Avenue, Suite 1800, Phoenix, Arizona 85004-3099	(602) 640-2160	(602) 640-2178	Cornele A. Overstreet
Region 29	One MetroTech Center, Jay Street and Myrtle Avenue, 10th Floor, Brooklyn, New York 11201-4201	(718) 330-7713	(718) 330-7579	Alvin P. Blyer
Region 30	Henry S. Reuss Federal Plaza, 310 W. Wisconsin Avenue, Suite 700, Milwaukee, Wisconsin 53203-2211	(414) 297-3861	(414) 297-3880	Philip E. Bloedorn
Region 31	11150 W. Olympic Blvd, Suite 700, Los Angeles, California 90064-1824	(310) 235-7352	(310) 235-7420	James J. McDermott
Region 32	1301 Clay Street, Room 300N, Oakland, California 94612-5211	(510) 637-3300	(510) 637-3315	Vacant
Subregion 33	300 Hamilton Boulevard, Suite 200, Peoria, Illinois 61602-1246	(309) 671-7080	(309) 671-7095	Will Vance
Region 34	280 Trumbull Street, 21st Floor, Hartford, Connecticut 06103-3599	(860) 240-3522	(860) 240-3564	Peter B. Hoffman

REGION	ADDRESS	TELEPHONE	FAX	REGIONAL DIRECTOR
Subregion 36	601 SW Second Ave., Suite 1910, Portland, Oregon 97204-3170	(503) 326-3085	(503) 326-5387	Cathleen Shelton
Subregion 37	300 Ala Moana Blvd., Room 7245, Honolulu, Hawaii 96850-4980	(808) 541-2814	(808) 541-2818	Thomas W. Cestare

APPENDIX 5:
NATIONAL LABOR RELATIONS BOARD—DIRECTORY OF RESIDENT OFFICES

JURISDICTION	ADDRESS	TELEPHONE	FAX	RESIDENT OFFICER
ALABAMA	3400 Ridge Park Place, Birmingham, Alabama 35205-2870	(205) 731-1062	(205) 731-0955	C. Douglas Marshall
ALASKA	1007 W. Third Avenue, Suite 206, Anchorage, Alaska 99501-1936	(907) 271-5015	(907) 271-3055	Minoru Hayashi
ARKANSAS	TCBY Tower, 425 West Capitol Avenue, Suite 375, Little Rock, Arkansas 72201-3489	(501) 324-6311	(501) 324-5009	Vacant
CALIFORNIA	555 W. Beech Street, Suite 418, San Diego, California 92101-2939	(619) 557-6184	(619) 557-6358	Steven J. Sorenson

JURISDICTION	ADDRESS	TELEPHONE	FAX	RESIDENT OFFICER
FLORIDA	Federal Building, 400 West Bay Street, Room 214, Jacksonville, Florida 32202-4412	(904) 232-3768	(904) 232-3146	James L. McDonald
FLORIDA	Federal Building, 51 SW. First Avenue, Room 1320, Miami, Florida 33130-1608	(305) 536-5391	(305) 536-5320	Hector O. Nava
IOWA	Federal Building, 210 Walnut Street, Room 439, Des Moines, Iowa 50309-2103	(515) 284-4391	(515) 284-4713	David Garza
MICHIGAN	82 Ionia NW, Room 330, Grand Rapids, Michigan 49503-3022	(616) 456-2679	(616) 456-2596	Chet H. Byerly, Jr.
NEVADA	600 Las Vegas Boulevard South, Suite 400, Las Vegas, Nevada 89101-6637	(702) 388-6416	(702) 388-6248	Michael Chavez
NEW MEXICO	505 Marquette Avenue, NW, Suite 1820, Albuquerque, New Mexico 87102-2181	(505) 248-5125	(505) 248-5134	Kathleen McCorkell

JURISDICTION	ADDRESS	TELEPHONE	FAX	RESIDENT OFFICER
NEW YORK	Leo W. O'Brien Federal Building, Clinton Avenue at North Pearl Street, Room 342, Albany, New York	(518) 431-4155	(518) 431-4157	Jon Mackle
OKLAHOMA	224 South Boulder Avenue, Room 318, Tulsa, Oklahoma 74103-3027	(918) 581-795	(918) 581-7970	Francis A. Molenda
TENNESSEE	810 Broadway, 3rd Floor, Nashville, Tennessee 37203-3816	(615) 736-5921	(615) 736-7761	Joseph H. Artiles
TEXAS	P.O. Box 23159, El Paso, Texas 79923	(915) 565-2470	(915) 565-0847	Chris D. Lerma
TEXAS	Mickey Leland Federal Building, 1919 Smith Street, Suite 1545, Houston, Texas 77002-2649	(713) 209-4888	(713) 209-4890	Nadine Littles
TEXAS	615 East Houston Street, San Antonio, Texas 78205-2040	(210) 472-6140	(210) 472-6143	Olivia Garcia Boult

JURISDICTION	ADDRESS	TELEPHONE	FAX	RESIDENT OFFICER
WASHINGTON D.C.	Franklin Court Building, 1099 14th Street, Suite 5530, Washington, D.C. 20570-0001	(202) 208-3000	(202) 208-3013	Mark Baptiste-Kalaris

APPENDIX 6:
NATIONAL LABOR RELATIONS BOARD—STAFF DIRECTORY

TITLE	NAME	TELEPHONE
CHAIRMAN	Peter J. Hurtgen	202-273-1770
Chief Counsel	Harold Datz	202-273-1770
Deputy Chief Counsel	David Martin	202-273-1770
Executive Assistant	Kathleen Nixon	202-273-1770
Special Assistant	Mary Meyers	202-273-1770
BOARD MEMBER	Wilma B. Liebman	202-273-1700
Chief Counsel	John F. Colwell	202-273-1700
Deputy Chief Counsel	Robert R. Richards	202-273-1700
Special Assistant	Diane H. Byrd	202-273-1700
BOARD MEMBER	William B. Cowen	202-273-1070
Chief Counsel (Acting)	Gary Shinners	202-273-1070
Deputy Chief Counsel	Robert F. Kane	202-273-1070
Special Assistant	Patricia Holt	202-273-1070
BOARD MEMBER	Michael J. Bartlett	202-273-1790
Chief Counsel (Acting)	Jeffrey D. Wedekind	202-273-1790
Deputy Chief Counsel	Alfred Wolff	202-273-1790
Special Assistant	Eileen Steffanick	202-273-1790
BOARD MEMBER	Vacant	202-273-1740
Chief Counsel (Acting)	Dennis P. Walsh	202-273-1740
Deputy Chief Counsel	Jonathan Scheinbart	202-273-1740

TITLE	NAME	TELEPHONE
Special Assistant	Mildred Corthon	202-273-1740
EXECUTIVE SECRETARY	John J. Toner	202-273-1940
Deputy Executive Secretary	Lester A. Heltzer	202-273-1940
Associate Executive Secretary	Enid W. Weber	202-273-1940
Associate Executive Secretary	Hollace J. Enoch	202-273-1940
Associate Executive Secretary	Richard D. Hardick	202-273-1940
Special Assistant	Mary E. Ebron	202-273-1940
Staff Assistant	Marianne Valaer	202-273-1940
Docket Order and Issuance Section Chief	Shirl Jackson	202-273-1940
SOLICITOR	Jeffrey D. Wedekind	202-273-2910
Associate Solicitor	Henry Breiteneicher	202-273-2910
Assistant Solicitor		202-273-2910
Assistant Solicitor	Susan Leverone	202-273-2910
Staff Assistant	Rosetta Moton	202-273-2910
INSPECTOR GENERAL	Jane E. Altenhofen	202-273-1960
Counsel to Inspector General	David P. Berry	202-273-1960
Special Agent	Kathryn L. Jones	202-273-1960
Supervisory Auditor	Emil T. George	202-273-1960
Auditor	Bridgette Hicks	202-273-1960
Auditor	Joyce N. Werking	202-273-1960
DIRECTOR, OFFICE OF REPRESENTATION APPEALS	Lafe Solomon	202-273-1980
Administrative Aide	Cynthia Turner	202-273-1980
DIRECTOR, DIVISION OF INFORMATION	David B. Parker	202-273-1991
Associate Director	Patricia Gilbert	202-273-1991
Public Inquiry Assistant	Sharon Y. Hodge	202-273-1991
CHIEF ADMINISTRATIVE LAW JUDGE	Robert A. Giannasi	202-501-8800
Deputy Chief Administrative Law Judge	Richard A. Scully	202-501-8800

TITLE	NAME	TELEPHONE
Associate Chief Administrative Law Judge	Vacant	202-501-8800
Staff Assistant	Anna Marie Wehausen	202-501-8800
Associate Chief Administrative Law Judge	William L. Schmidt	415-356-5255
Office Manager	Susan H. George	415-356-5255
Associate Chief Administrative Law Judge	Joel P. Biblowitz	212-944-2941
Office Manager	Wanda Blakemore	212-944-2941
Associate Chief Administrative Law Judge	William N. Cates	404-331-6652
Office Manager	Willene Heflin	404-331-6652
GENERAL COUNSEL	Arthur F. Rosenfeld	202-273-3700
Confidential Staff Assistant	Ernestine Contee	202-273-3700
Deputy General Counsel (Acting)	John E. Higgins, Jr.	202-273-3700
Assistant General Counsel	Joseph F. Frankl	202- 273-3700
DIRECTOR, OFFICE OF EMPLOYEE DEVELOPMENT	Tom Christman	202-273-3914
DIRECTOR, EQUAL EMPLOYMENT OPPORTUNITY	Robert J. Poindexter	202-273-3891
Deputy Director	Lori Suto-Goldsby	202-273-0761
EEO Specialist	Felicia Toney	202-273-3892
ASSOCIATE GENERAL COUNSEL	Richard A. Siegel	202-273-2900
Staff Assistant	Cassandra M. Saunders	202-273-2900
Deputy Associate General Counsel	Anne Purcell	202-273-2900
ASSISTANT GENERAL COUNSEL, District I	James G. Paulsen	202-273-2881
Deputy Associate General Counsel	Helen E. Marsh	202-273-2881
Deputy Associate General Counsel	Elizabeth Kirkpatrick	202-273-2881

TITLE	NAME	TELEPHONE
ASSISTANT GENERAL COUNSEL, District II	Jane C. Schnabel	202-273-2885
Deputy Associate General Counsel	Gary Muffley	202-273-2885
Deputy Associate General Counsel	Louis Cimmino	(913) 967-3003
ASSISTANT GENERAL COUNSEL, District III	Charles L. Posner	202-273-2889
Deputy Associate General Counsel	Shelley S. Korch	202-273-2889
Deputy Associate General Counsel	Hugo Voogd	202-273-2889
ASSISTANT GENERAL COUNSEL, District IV	Nelson A. Levin	202-273-2893
Deputy Associate General Counsel	Joseph J. Baniszewski	202-273-2893
Deputy Associate General Counsel	Yvette Hatfield	202-2732893
Assistant General Counsel, Labor & Employee Relations	Harry E. Jones	202-273-2886
Executive Assistant	Carole K. Coleman	202-273-2901
Special Assistant	Nancy E. Krystkiewicz	202-273-2901
Special Counsel to the General Counsel	Peter A. Eveleth	202-273-2878
Special Counsel to the General Counsel	Jennifer S. Kovachich	202-273-3781
Special Counsel to the General Counsel	Barry F. Smith	202-273-2898
Special Counsel to the General Counsel	Joseph M. Davis	202-273-2722
ASSOCIATE GENERAL COUNSEL, DIVISION OF ADVICE	Barry J. Kearney	202-273-3800
Staff Assistant	Dawn M. Nelson	202-273-3800
Secretarial Assistant	Robyn R. Person	202-273-3800
Deputy Associate General Counsel	Ellen A. Farrell	202-273-3800

TITLE	NAME	TELEPHONE
Assistant General Counsel	David Colangelo	202-273-3831
Deputy Assistant General Counsel	Alan Fener	202-273-3824
Assistant General Counsel, Injunction Litigation	Judith I. Katz	202-273-3810
Deputy Assistant General Counsel	Peter B. Mirsky	202-273-3811
Assistant General Counsel, Research and Policy Planning	John W. Hornbeck	202-273-3847
Head, Legal Research Section	Beryl M. Rothman	202-273-3848
Head, Legal Retrieval & Publication Section	Herbert E. Weiser	202-273-3849
ASSOCIATE GENERAL COUNSEL, DIVISION OF ENFORCEMENT LITIGATION	John H. Ferguson	202-273-2950
Staff Assistant	Brenda B. Banks	202-273-2950
Secretarial Assistant	Victoria A. Thomas	202-273-2950
Deputy Associate General Counsel, Appellate Court Branch	Aileen Armstrong	202-273-2960
Deputy Branch Chief	Linda Dreeben	202-273-2966
Assistant General Counsel	Vacant	202-273-2977
Deputy Assistant General Counsel	Howard E. Perlstein	202-273-2946
Deputy Assistant General Counsel	Peter Winkler	202-273-2982
Chief, Litigation Services	Barbara A. Blackwell	202-273-3860
Assistant General Counsel (Acting), Contempt Litigation and Compliance Branch	Stanley Zirkin	202-273-3737
Deputy Assistant General Counsel	Daniel Collopy	202-273-3739
Assistant General Counsel, Special Litigation Branch	Margery E. Lieber	202-273-2930
Deputy Assistant General Counsel	Eric G. Moskowitz	202-273-2931

TITLE	NAME	TELEPHONE
Deputy Associate General Counsel, Supreme Court Branch	Norton J. Come	202-273-2954
DIRECTOR, OFFICE OF APPEALS	Yvonne T. Dixon	202-273-3760
Assistant Director	Deborah M. P. Yaffe	202-273-3760
DIRECTOR, DIVISION OF ADMINISTRATION	Gloria J. Joseph	202-273-3890
Deputy Director	Frank V. Battle	202-273-3890
Chief, Security Branch	Eugene Lott, Jr.	202-273-1990
Chief, Library and Administrative Services Branch	Vanita C.S. Reynolds	202-273-3920
CIO, Information Technology Branch	Louis B. Adams	202-273-4030
Deputy CIO	Patsy B. Davis	204-273-3903
Chief (Information Systems Section)	Marilyn Collins	202- 273-4138
Chief (Information Infrastructure Section)	Francis X. Young	202-273-4032
Chief (Customer Support Section)	Bette Y. Mohr	202-273-4066
Chief (Program Management Staff)	Henrietta Brox	202-273-0731
Director, Personnel Branch	Catherine McCoy	202-273-3900
Chief, Procurement and Facilities Branch	Angela Crawford	202-273-4040
Assistant Branch Chief	Sydney A. Lee	202-273-4040
Chief (Acting), Budget Branch	Lisa Bevels	202-273-3970
Assistant Chief	Vacant	202-273-3907
Chief, Finance Branch	Karl Rohrbaugh	202-273-4230
President, NLRB Professional Association	Leslie Rossen	202-273-1749
Vice President	Anne Marie Lofaso	202-273-2985
Secretary	Karen Cook-Landon	202-273-1086
Treasurer	Tom Clark	202-273-1979

TITLE	NAME	TELEPHONE
General Counsel Grievance Chair	Joan Sullivan	202-273-3742
Board Grievance Chair	Nora Carroll	202-273-1922
Legislative and Public Affairs	David Seddelmeyer	202-273-3771
President, NLRBU Executive Committee	D. Bruce Hill (Peoria)	309-671-7093
Vice President	Eric Brooks (Manhattan)	212-264-0319
Secretary	A. Marie Simpson (Minneapolis)	612-348-1795
Treasurer	Deborah K. Rogers (Minneapolis)	612-348-1769
Grievance Chairperson	Doren G. Goldstone (Buffalo)	716-551-4952
Support Staff Representative	Diane C. Walthall (Denver)	303-844-6652
NLRBU District Vice-President, District A (Locals 1, 2, 4, 22, 29, and 34)	Burt Pearlstone (Manhattan)	212-2643040
NLRBU District Vice-President, District B (Locals 3, 6, 7, 8, 9, 23 and 25)	Natalie D. Morton (Cincinnati)	513-684-3724
NLRBU District Vice-President, District C (Locals 5, 10, 11, 12, 15, 24 and 26)	Dallas Manuel (Tampa)	813-228-2669
NLRBU District Vice-President, District D (Locals 13, 14, 16, 17, 18, 27, 30 and 33)	Ethan Ray (Chicago)	312-353-9164
NLRBU District Vice-President, District E (Locals 19, 20, 21, 28, 31, 32, 36 and 37)	Virginia Jordan (Oakland)	510-637-3287
NLRBU District Vice-President, Washington (Washington Local & Division of Judges)	Vanise Lee (San Francisco)	415-356-5256
NLRBU Committee, EEO	Greg Davis (Manhattan)	212-264-0342
NLRBU Committee, Health and Safety	David Biggar (Minneapolis)	612-348-1773

TITLE	NAME	TELEPHONE
NLRBU Committee, Legislative	Jon H. Grove (Cincinnati)	513-684-3750
NLRBU Committee, Membership	Margarita Navarro-Rivera (Philadelphia)	215-597-7647
NLRBU Committee, Remedy	Richard F. Czubaj (Detroit)	313-226-3214
NLRBU Committee, Training	Olga Bestilny (Minneapolis)	612-348-1790
President, Washington Local	Willie Mae Thorpe	202-273-3753
Vice President (GC), Washington Local	Loretta Jackson	202-273-4064
Vice President (Board), Washington Local	Burnetta Hight	202-273-1739
Corresponding Secretary, Washington Local	Gladys Johnson	202-273-4038
Recording Secretary, Washington Local	vacant	n/a
Treasurer, Washington Local	vacant	n/a
Sergeant-at-Arms, Washington Local	Gwen Hill	202-273-3965
Sergeant-at-Arms, Washington Local	Maurice Morton	202-273-3964

APPENDIX 7:
DIRECTORY OF STATE DEPARTMENTS OF LABOR

STATE	ADDRESS	TELEPHONE	FAX	INTERNET ADDRESS
ALABAMA	Department of Labor, P.O. Box 303500, Montgomery, AL 36130-3500	334-242-3460	334-240-3417	www.dir.state.al.us
ALASKA	Department of Labor, P.O. Box 21149, Juneau, AK 99802-1149	907-465-2700	907-465-2784	www.labor.state.ak.us
ARIZONA	State Labor Department, P.O. Box 19070, Phoenix, AZ 85005-9070	602-542-4411	602-542-3104	www.ica.state.az.us
ARKANSAS	Department of Labor, 10421 West Markham, Little Rock, AR 72205	501-682-4541	501-682-4535	www.state.ar.us/labor

STATE	ADDRESS	TELEPHONE	FAX	INTERNET ADDRESS
CALIFORNIA	Department of Industrial Relations, 455 Golden Gate Ave., 10th Floor, San Francisco, CA 94102	415-703-5050	415-703-5059	www.dir.ca. gov
COLORADO	Department of Labor and Employment, 2 Park Central, Suite 400, Denver, CO 80202-2117	303-620-4701	303-620-4714	http://cdle.s tate.co.us
CONNECTI-CUT	Labor Department, 200 Folly Brook Boulevard, Wethersfield, CT 06109-1114	860-263-6505	860-263-6529	www.ctdol.s tate.ct.us
DELAWARE	Department of Labor, 4425 N. Market Street, 4th Floor.. Wilmington, DE 19802	302-761-8000	302-761-6621	Www.delaw areworks. com
DISTRICT OF COLUMBIA	Department of Employment Services, Employment Security Building, 500 "C" Street NW, Suite 600, Washington, D.C. 20001	202-724-7100	202-724-5683	does.ci.was hington.dc. us

STATE	ADDRESS	TELEPHONE	FAX	INTERNET ADDRESS
FLORIDA	Department of Labor and Employment Security, 2012 Capitol Circle S.E., Hartman Building, Suite 303, Tallahassee, FL 32399-2152	850-922-7021	904-488-8930	www.state.fl.us/dles
GEORGIA	Department of Labor, Sussex Place—Room 600, 148 International Blvd. N.E., Atlanta, GA 30303	404-656-3011	404-656-2683	www.dol.state.ga.us
HAWAII	Department of Labor and Industrial Relations, 830 Punchbowl Street, Room 321, Honolulu, HI 96813	808-586-8844	808-586-9099	www.dlir.state.hi.us
IDAHO	Department of Labor, 317 W. Main Street, Boise, ID 83735-0001	208-334-6110	208-334-6430	www.labor.state.id.us
ILLINOIS	Department of Labor, 160 N. LaSalle Street, 13th Floor, Suite C-1300, Chicago, IL 60601	312-793-1808	312-793-5257	www.state.il.us/agency/idol

STATE	ADDRESS	TELEPHONE	FAX	INTERNET ADDRESS
INDIANA	Department of Labor, 402 West Washington Street, Room W195, Indianapolis, IN 46204-2739	317-232-2378	317-233-5381	www.state. in.us/labor
IOWA	Iowa Workforce Development, 1000 East Grand Avenue, Des Moines, IA 50319-0209	515-281-5365	515-281-4698	www.state. ia.us/iwd
KANSAS	Department of Human Resources, 401 S.W. Topeka Boulevard, Topeka, KS 66603	785-296-7474	785-368-6294	www.hr. state.ks.us
KENTUCKY	Kentucky Labor Cabinet, 1047 U.S. Hwy. 127 South, Suite 4, Frankfort, KY 40601	502-564-3070	502-564-5387	www.state. ky.us/agen cies/labor/la brhome.htm
LOUISIANA	Department of Labor, P.O. Box 94094, Baton Rouge, LA 70804-9094	225-342-3011	225-342-3778	www.ldol. state.la.us
MAINE	Department of Labor, 20 Union Street, P.O. Box 259, Augusta, ME 04332-0259	207-287-3788	207-287-5292	

STATE	ADDRESS	TELEPHONE	FAX	INTERNET ADDRESS
	Bureau of Labor Standards, Department of Labor, State House Station #45, Augusta, ME 04333	207-624-6400	207-624-6449	http://janus. state.me.us/ labor
MARYLAND	Department of Labor, Licensing and Regulation, 500 N. Calvert Street, Suite 401, Baltimore, MD 21202	410-230-6020 ext. 1393	410-333-0853 or 410-333-1229	
	Department of Labor, Licensing and Regulation, Division of Labor and Industry, 1100 Eutaw St. 6th Floor, Baltimore, MD 21201	410-767-2999	410-767-2986	www.dllr. state.md.us
MASSACHU-SETTS	Department of Labor & Work Force Development, 1 Ashburton Place, Rm 2112, Boston, MA 02108	617-727-6573	617-727-1090	www. detma.org/ index.htm or www.state. ma.us
MICHIGAN	Department of Consumer & Industry Services, P.O. Box 30004, Lansing, MI 48909	517-373-3034	517-373-2129	www.cis. state.mi. us/bsr/ divisions/ whd/home. htm

STATE	ADDRESS	TELEPHONE	FAX	INTERNET ADDRESS
MICHIGAN	Department of Consumer & Industry Services, P.O. Box 30004, Lansing, MI 48909	517-373-3034	517-373-2129	www.cis. state.mi. us/bsr/ divisions/ whd/home. htm
MINNESOTA	Department of Labor and Industry, 443 Lafayette Road, St. Paul, MN 55155	651-296-2342	651-282-5405	www.doli. state.mn.us
MISSISSIPPI	Executive Director, Employment Security Commission, P.O. Box 1699, Jackson, MS 39215-1699	601-961-7400	601-961-7406	www.mesc. state.ms.us
	Chairman, Workers' Compensation Commission, 1428 Lakeland Drive, P.O. Box 5300, Jackson, MS 39296	601-987-4258	601-987-4233	www.mwcc. state.ms.us
MISSOURI	Chairman, Labor and Industrial Relations Commission, P.O. Box 599, 3315 W. Truman Boulevard, Jefferson City, MO 65102	573-751-2461	573-751-7806	

STATE	ADDRESS	TELEPHONE	FAX	INTERNET ADDRESS
	Members of the Commission, Labor and Industrial Relations Commission, P.O. Box 599, Jefferson City, MO 65102	573-751-2461	573-751-7806	
	Department of Labor & Industrial Relations, P.O. Box 504, Jefferson City, MO 65102	573-751-9691	573-751-4135	www.solir. state.mo.us
MONTANA	Department of Labor and Industry, P.O. Box 1728, Helena, MT 59624-1728	406-444-9091	406-444-1394	http://dli. state.mt.us
NEBRASKA	Department of Labor, 550 South 16th Street, Box 94600, Lincoln, NE 68509-4600	402-471-9792	402-471-2318	www.dol. state.ne.us/
NEVADA	Business and Industry, 555 E. Washington Avenue, Suite 4100, Las Vegas, NV 89101	702-486-2650	702-486-2660	www.state. nv.us/labor
NEW HAMPSHIRE	Department of Labor, 95 Pleasant Street, Concord, NH 03301	603-271-3171	603-271-6852	www.state. nh.us/dol

STATE	ADDRESS	TELEPHONE	FAX	INTERNET ADDRESS
NEW JERSEY	New Jersey Dept. of Labor, John Fitch Plaza, 13th Floor, Suite D, P.O. Box CN 110, Trenton, NJ 08625-0110	609-292-2323	609-633-9271	www.state. nj.us/labor
NEW MEXICO	Department of Labor, P.O. Box 1928, 401 Broadway, N.E., Albuquerque, NM 87103-1928	505-841-8408	505-841-8491	www3. state.nm. us/dol
NEW YORK	Commissiner, Department of Labor, State Campus, Building 12, Albany, NY 12240 -or-	518-457-2741	518-457-6908	
	345 Hudson Street, New York, NY 10014-0675	212-352-6000		www.labor. state.ny.us
NORTH CAROLINA	Department of Labor, 4 West Edenton Street, Raleigh, NC 27601-1092	919-733-0360	919-733-6197	Www.dol. state.nc.us

STATE	ADDRESS	TELEPHONE	FAX	INTERNET ADDRESS
NORTH DAKOTA	Department of Labor, State Capitol Building, 600 East Boulevard, Dept. 406, Bismark, ND 58505-0340	701-328-2660	701-328-2031	www.state. nd.us/labor
OHIO	Department of Commerce, 77 South High St., 23rd Floor, Columbus, OH 43266	614-466-7053	614-466-5650	Http://www. state.oh.us/ ohio/ agency.htm
OKLAHOMA	Department of Labor, 4001 N. Lincoln Blvd., Oklahoma City, OK 73105-5212	405-528-1500	405-528-5751	www.state. ok.us/~ok dol
OREGON	Bureau of Labor and Industries, 800 NE Oregon Street #32, Portland, OR 97232	503-731-4070	503-7314103	www.boli. state.or.us
PENNSYLVA-NIA	Department of Labor and Industry, 1700 Labor and Industry Building, 7th and Forster Streets, Harrisburg, PA 17120	717-787-3756	717-787-8826	www.li. state.pa.us
RHODE ISLAND	Department of Labor and Training, 1511 Pontiac Avenue, Cranston, RI 02920	401-462-8870	401-462-8872	www.det. state.ri.us

STATE	ADDRESS	TELEPHONE	FAX	INTERNET ADDRESS
SOUTH CAROLINA	Department of Labor, Synergy Center—King St. Building, 110 Center View Drive, P.O. Box 11329, Columbia, SC 29211-1329	803-896-4300	803-896-4393	www.llr. state.sc.us
SOUTH DAKOTA	Department of Labor, 700 Governors Drive, Pierre, SD 57501-2291	605-773-3101	605-773-4211	www.state. Sd.us/dol/ dol.htm
TENNESSEE	Department of Labor, Andrew Johnson Tower, 710 James Robertson Pky., 8th Floor, Nashville, TN 37243-0655	615-741-6642	615-741-5078	www.state. tn.us
TEXAS	Texas Workforce Commission, 101 East 15th Street, Rm 618, Austin, TX 78778	512-463-0735	512-475-2321	www.twc. state.tx.us
UTAH	Utah Labor Commission, P.O. Box 146600, Salt Lake City, UT 84111-2316	801-530-6880	801-530-6390	www.labor. state.ut.us

STATE	ADDRESS	TELEPHONE	FAX	INTERNET ADDRESS
VERMONT	Department of Labor & Industry, National Life Building, Drawer #20, Montpelier, VT 05620-3401	802-828-2288	802-828-0408	www.state. vt.us/labind
VIRGINIA	Dept. of Labor and Industry, Powers-Taylor Building, 13 S. 13th, Richmond, VA 23219	804-786-2377	804-371-6524	www.dli. state.va.us
WASHING-TON	Department of Labor & Industries, P.O. Box 44001, Olympia, WA 98504-4001	360-902-4213	360-902-4202	www.wa. gov/lni
WEST VIRGINIA	Division of Labor, State Capitol Complex, Building #3, Room 319, Charleston, WV 25305	304-558-7890	304-558-3797	www.state. wv.us/labor
WISCONSIN	Department of Workforce Development, 201 East Washington Avenue, #400, P.O. Box 7946, Madison, WI 53707-7946	608-266-7552	608-266-1784	www.dwd. state.wi.us

STATE	ADDRESS	TELEPHONE	FAX	INTERNET ADDRESS
WYOMING	Department of Employment, Herschler Building, 2-East, 122 W. 25th Street, Cheyenne, WY 82002	307-777-7672	307-777-5805	http://wy doe.state. wy.us/ labstd

APPENDIX 8:
NLRB REPRESENTATION PETITION

PLEASE REVIEW THE FOLLOWING IMPORTANT INFORMATION BEFORE FILLING OUT A PETITION FORM!

- Please call an Information Officer in the Regional Office nearest you for assistance in filing a petition. The Information Officer will be happy to answer your questions about the petition form or to draft the petition on your behalf.
- Check one of the boxes listed under Question 1 representing the purpose of the petition: RC-a union desires to be certified as the bargaining representative of employees; RM-an employer seeks an election because one or more individuals or unions have sought recognition as the bargaining representative, or based on a reasonable belief supported by objective considerations that the currently recognized union has lost its majority status; RD-employees seek to remove the currently recognized union as the bargaining representative; UD-employees desire an election to restrict the union's right to maintain a union shop clause; UC-a labor organization or an employer seeks clarification of the existing bargaining unit; or AC-a labor organization or an employer seeks an amendment of a certification issued in a prior Board case.
- Under Question 5, please carefully describe the bargaining unit involved in the petition, listing the job classifications included in the unit and the job classifications excluded from the unit.
- After completing the petition form, be sure to sign and date the petition and mail, fax or hand deliver the completed petition form to the appropriate Regional Office.
- The filing of a petition seeking certification or decertification of a union should be accompanied by a sufficient showing of interest to support such a petition—i.e., a showing that 30% or more of the employees in the bargaining unit seek to be represented by the union or seek to decertify the currently recognized union. If the original showing is not sent to the Region with the filing of the petition, a party must deliver the original showing of interest to the Region within **48 hours** after the filing of the petition, but in no event later than the last day on which a petition may be timely filed.
- Be sure to include telephone and fax numbers of the parties since this will be a significant aid to the processing of the petition.
- Be sure to include the name and address of any other labor organization or individuals known to have a representative interest in any of the employees in the unit described in Question 5 of the petition.
- A petition should be filed with the Regional Office where the bargaining unit exists. If the bargaining unit exists in two or more Regions, it can be filed in any of such Regions. An Information Officer will be happy to assist you in locating the appropriate Regional Office in which to file your petition.

NLRB REPRESENTATION PETITION

FORM NLRB-502 (3-96)	UNITED STATES GOVERNMENT NATIONAL LABOR RELATIONS BOARD PETITION	FORM EXEMPT UNDER 44 U.S.C. 3512		
		DO NOT WRITE IN THIS SPACE		
		Case No.		Date Filed

INSTRUCTIONS: Submit an original and 4 copies of this Petition to the NLRB Regional Office in the Region in which the employer concerned is located. If more space is required for any one item, attach additional sheets, numbering item accordingly.

The Petitioner alleges that the following circumstances exist and requests that the National Labor Relations Board proceed under its proper authority pursuant to Section 9 of the National Labor Relations Act.

1. **PURPOSE OF THIS PETITION** *(If box RC, RM, or RD is checked and a charge under Section 8(b)(7) of the Act has been filed involving the Employer named herein, the statement following the description of the type of petition shall not be deemed made.)* **(Check One)**

   ☐ **RC-CERTIFICATION OF REPRESENTATIVE** - A substantial number of employees wish to be represented for purposes of collective bargaining by Petitioner and Petitioner desires to be certified as representative of the employees.

   ☐ **RM-REPRESENTATION (EMPLOYER PETITION)** - One or more individuals or labor organizations have presented a claim to Petitioner to be recognized as the representative of employees of Petitioner.

   ☐ **RD-DECERTIFICATION (REMOVAL OF REPRESENTATIVE)** - A substantial number of employees assert that the certified or currently recognized bargaining representative is no longer their representative.

   ☐ **UD-WITHDRAWAL OF UNION SHOP AUTHORITY (REMOVAL OF OBLIGATION TO PAY DUES)** - Thirty percent (30%) or more of employees in a bargaining unit covered by an agreement between their employer and a labor organization desire that such authority be rescinded.

   ☐ **UC-UNIT CLARIFICATION** - A labor organization is currently recognized by Employer, but Petitioner seeks clarification of placement of certain employees: *(Check one)* ☐ In unit not previously certified. ☐ In unit previously certified in Case No. _____

   ☐ **AC-AMENDMENT OF CERTIFICATION** - Petitioner seeks amendment of certification issued in Case No. _____
   Attach statement describing the specific amendment sought.

2. Name of Employer	Employer Representative to contact	Telephone Number

3. Address(es) of Establishment(s) involved *(Street and number, city, State, ZIP code)*	Telecopier Number (Fax)

4a. Type of Establishment *(Factory, mine, wholesaler, etc.)*	4b. Identify principal product or service

5. Unit involved *(in UC petition, describe present bargaining unit and attached description of proposed clarification.)*	6a. Number of Employees in Unit:
Included	Present
	Proposed *(By UC/AC)*
Excluded	6b. Is this petition supported by 30% or more of the employees in the unit?* ☐ Yes ☐ No
(If you have checked box RC in 1 above, check and complete EITHER item 7a or 7b, whichever is applicable.)	*Not applicable in RM, UC, and AC

7a.	☐	Request for recognition as Bargaining Representative was made on *(Date)* _____ and Employer declined recognition on or about *(Date)* _____ *(If no reply received, so state.)*
7b.	☐	Petitioner is currently recognized as Bargaining Representative and desires certification under the Act.

8. Name of Recognized or Certified Bargaining Agent *(If none, so state.)*	Affiliation

Address, Telephone No. and Telecopier No. (Fax)	Date of Recognition or Certification

9. Expiration Date of Current Contract, If any *(Month, Day, Year)*	10. If you have checked box UD in 1 above, show here the date of execution of agreement granting union shop *(Month, Day, and Year)*

11a. Is there now a strike or picketing at the Employer's establishment(s) involved? Yes _____ No _____	11b. If so, approximately how many employees are participating?

11c. The Employer has been picketed by or on behalf of *(Insert Name)* _____, a labor organization, of *(Insert Address)* _____ Since *(Month, Day, Year)* _____

12. Organizations or individuals other than Petitioner (and other than those named in items 8 and 11c), which have claimed recognition as representatives and other organizations and individuals known to have a representative interest in any employees in unit described in item 5 above. *(If none, so state.)*

Name	Affiliation	Address	Date of Claim
			Telecopier No. (Fax)

13. Full name of party filing petition (If labor organization, give full name, including local name and number)

14a. Address *(street and number, city, state, and ZIP code)*	14b. Telephone No.
	14c. Telecopier No. (Fax)

15. Full name of national or international labor organization of which it is an affiliate or constituent unit *(to be filled in when petition is filed by a labor organization)*

I declare that I have read the above petition and that the statements are true to the best of my knowledge and belief.

Name *(Print)*	Signature	Title *(if any)*
Address *(street and number, city, state, and ZIP code)*		Telephone No.
		Telecopier No. (Fax)

WILLFUL FALSE STATEMENTS ON THIS PETITION CAN BE PUNISHED BY FINE AND IMPRISONMENT (U.S. CODE, TITLE 18, SECTION 1001)

APPENDIX 9:
NLRB UNFAIR LABOR PRACTICE CHARGE FORM

Please Review the Following
Important Information
Before Filling Out a Charge Form!

- Please call an Information Officer in the Regional Office nearest you for assistance in filing a charge. The Information Officer will be happy to answer your questions about the charge form or to draft the charge on your behalf. Seeking assistance from an Information Officer may help you to avoid having the processing of your charge delayed or your charge dismissed because of mistakes made in completing the form.

- Please be advised that not every workplace action that you may view as unfair constitutes an unfair labor practice within the jurisdiction of the National Labor Relations Act (NLRA). Please click on the Help Desk button for more information on matters covered by the NLRA.

- The section of the charge form called, "Basis of Charge," seeks only a brief description of the alleged unfair labor practice. You should **NOT** include a detailed recounting of the evidence in support of the charge or a list of the names and telephone numbers of witnesses.

- After completing the charge form, be sure to sign and date the charge and mail or deliver the completed form to the appropriate Regional Office.

- A charge should be filed with the Regional Office which has jurisdiction over the geographic area of the United States where the unfair labor practice occurred. For example, an unfair labor practice charge alleging that an employer unlawfully discharged an employee would usually be filed with the Regional Office having jurisdiction over the worksite where the employee was employed prior to his/her discharge. An Information Officer will be pleased to assist you in locating the appropriate Regional Office in which to file your charge.

- The NLRB's Rules and Regulations state that it is the responsibility of the individual, employer or union filing a charge to timely and properly serve a copy of the charge on the person, employer or union against whom such charge is made.

- By statute, only charges filed and served within **six (6) months** of the date of the event or conduct, which is the subject of that charge, will be processed by the NLRB.

NLRB UNFAIR LABOR PRACTICE CHARGE FORM

FORM NLRB-509
(5-89)

UNITED STATES OF AMERICA

FORM EXEMPT UNDER
44 U.S.C. 3512

NATIONAL LABOR RELATIONS BOARD

CHARGE ALLEGING UNFAIR LABOR PRACTICE UNDER SECTION 8(e) OF THE NLRA

INSTRUCTIONS: File an original and 3 copies of this charge, and an additional copy for each organization, each local, and each individual named in item 1 with the NLRB Regional Director for the region in which the alleged unfair labor practice occurred or is occurring.

CASE NUMBER	DATED FILED	1. CHARGE FILED AGAINST:		
		Employer and Labor Organization	Employer	Labor Organization

a. Name of Labor Organization (Give full name, including local name and number)	b. Union Representative to Contact	c. Telephone Number

d. Address (Street and number, city, State, and ZIP Code)

e. Name of Employer	f. Employer Representative to Contact	g. Telephone Number

h. Location of Plant Involved (Street, city, State, and ZIP Code)

i. Type of Establishment (Factory, mine, wholesaler, etc.)	j. Identify Principal Product or Service	k. No. of Workers Employed

The above-named labor organization or its agents, and/or employer(s) has (have) engaged in and is (are) engaging in unfair labor practices within the meaning of section 8(e) of the National Labor Relations Act, and these unfair labor practices are unfair labor practices affecting commerce within the meaning of the Act.

2. Basis of the Charge (Be specific about facts, names, plants involved, dates, and places.)

3. Full Name of Party Filing Charge (If labor organization, give full name, including local name and number)

a. Address (Street and number, city, State, and ZIP Code)	b. Telephone Number

4. Full Name of National or International Labor Organization of Which It is an Affiliate or Constituent Unit (To be filled in when charge is filed by a labor organization)

5. DECLARATION

I declare that I have read the above charge and that the statements therein are true to the best of my knowledge and belief.

By (Type/Print name of representative or person filing charge)	Title, if any	Telephone Number
Address	Signature	Date

APPENDIX 10:
NLRB UNFAIR LABOR PRACTICE FORM AGAINST AN EMPLOYER

Please Review the Following
Important Information
Before Filling Out a Charge Form!

- Please call an Information Officer in the Regional Office nearest you for assistance in filing a charge. The Information Officer will be happy to answer your questions about the charge form or to draft the charge on your behalf. Seeking assistance from an Information Officer may help you to avoid having the processing of your charge delayed or your charge dismissed because of mistakes made in completing the form.
- Please be advised that not every workplace action that you may view as unfair constitutes an unfair labor practice within the jurisdiction of the National Labor Relations Act (NLRA). Please click on the Help Desk button for more information on matters covered by the NLRA.
- The section of the charge form called, "Basis of Charge," seeks only a brief description of the alleged unfair labor practice. You should **NOT** include a detailed recounting of the evidence in support of the charge or a list of the names and telephone numbers of witnesses.
- After completing the charge form, be sure to sign and date the charge and mail or deliver the completed form to the appropriate Regional Office.
- A charge should be filed with the Regional Office which has jurisdiction over the geographic area of the United States where the unfair labor practice occurred. For example, an unfair labor practice charge alleging that an employer unlawfully discharged an employee would usually be filed with the Regional Office having jurisdiction over the worksite where the employee was employed prior to his/her discharge. An Information Officer will be pleased to assist you in locating the appropriate Regional Office in which to file your charge.
- The NLRB's Rules and Regulations state that it is the responsibility of the individual, employer or union filing a charge to timely and properly serve a copy of the charge on the person, employer or union against whom such charge is made.
- By statute, only charges filed and served within **six (6) months** of the date of the event or conduct, which is the subject of that charge, will be processed by the NLRB.

FORM NLRB-501
(11-94)

UNITED STATES OF AMERICA
NATIONAL LABOR RELATIONS BOARD
CHARGE AGAINST EMPLOYER

FORM EXEMPT UNDER 44 U.S.C. 3512

DO NOT WRITE IN THIS SPACE	
Case	Date Filed

INSTRUCTIONS:
File an original and 4 copies of this charge with NLRB Regional Director for the region in which the alleged unfair labor practice occurred or is occurring.

1. EMPLOYER AGAINST WHOM CHARGE IS BROUGHT		
a. Name of Employer		b. Number of Workers Employed
c. Address (street, city, State, ZIP, Code)	d. Employer Representative	e. Telephone No. / Fax No.
f. Type of Establishment (factory, mine, wholesaler, etc.)	g. Identify Principal Product or Service	

h. The above-named employer has engaged in and is engaging in unfair labor practices within the meaning of Section 8(a), subsections (1) and (list subsections) _____ of the National Labor Relations Act, and these unfair labor practices are unfair practices affecting commerce within the meaning of the Act.

2. Basis of the Charge (set forth a clear and concise statement of the facts constituting the alleged unfair labor practices.)

By the above and other acts, the above-named employer has interfered with, restrained, and coerced employees in the exercise of the rights guaranteed in Section 7 of the Act.

3. Full name of party filing charge (if labor organization, give full name, including local name and number)

4a. Address (street and number, city, State, and ZIP Code)	4b. Telephone No. / Fax No.

5. Full name of national or international labor organization of which it is an affiliate or constituent unit (to be filled in when charge is filed by a labor organization)

6. DECLARATION
I declare that I have read the above charge and that the statements are true to the best of my knowledge and belief.

By _____
(Signature of representative or person making charge)

Fax No. _____

_____
(Title, if any)

Address _____

_____
(Telephone No.)

_____
Date

WILLFUL FALSE STATEMENTS ON THIS CHARGE CAN BE PUNISHED BY FINE AND IMPRISONMENT (U.S. CODE, TITLE 18, SECTION 1001)

APPENDIX 11:
NLRB UNFAIR LABOR PRACTICE FORM
AGAINST A LABOR ORGANIZATION

Please Review the Following
Important Information
Before Filling Out a Charge Form!

- Please call an Information Officer in the Regional Office nearest you for assistance in filing a charge. The Information Officer will be happy to answer your questions about the charge form or to draft the charge on your behalf. Seeking assistance from an Information Officer may help you to avoid having the processing of your charge delayed or your charge dismissed because of mistakes made in completing the form.

- Please be advised that not every workplace action that you may view as unfair constitutes an unfair labor practice within the jurisdiction of the National Labor Relations Act (NLRA). Please click on the Help Desk button for more information on matters covered by the NLRA.

- The section of the charge form called, "Basis of Charge," seeks only a brief description of the alleged unfair labor practice. You should **NOT** include a detailed recounting of the evidence in support of the charge or a list of the names and telephone numbers of witnesses.

- After completing the charge form, be sure to sign and date the charge and mail or deliver the completed form to the appropriate Regional Office.

- A charge should be filed with the Regional Office which has jurisdiction over the geographic area of the United States where the unfair labor practice occurred. For example, an unfair labor practice charge alleging that an employer unlawfully discharged an employee would usually be filed with the Regional Office having jurisdiction over the worksite where the employee was employed prior to his/her discharge. An Information Officer will be pleased to assist you in locating the appropriate Regional Office in which to file your charge.

- The NLRB's Rules and Regulations state that it is the responsibility of the individual, employer or union filing a charge to timely and properly serve a copy of the charge on the person, employer or union against whom such charge is made.

- By statute, only charges filed and served within **six (6) months** of the date of the event or conduct, which is the subject of that charge, will be processed by the NLRB.

NLRB UNFAIR LABOR PRACTICE FORM AGAINST A LABOR ORGANIZATION

FORM NLRB-508
(6-90)

FORM EXEMPT UNDER 44 U.S.C. 3512

UNITED STATES OF AMERICA
NATIONAL LABOR RELATIONS BOARD
**CHARGE AGAINST LABOR ORGANIZATION
OR ITS AGENTS**

DO NOT WRITE IN THIS SPACE

Case	Date Filed

INSTRUCTIONS: File an original and 4 copies of this charge and an additional copy for each organization, each local, and each individual named in item 1 with the NLRB Regional Director of the region in which the alleged unfair labor practice occurred or is occurring.

1. LABOR ORGANIZATION OR ITS AGENTS AGAINST WHICH CHARGE IS BROUGHT

a. Name

b. Union Representative to contact

c. Telephone No.

d. Address (street, city, state and ZIP code)

e. The above-named organization(s) or its agents has (have) engaged in and is (are) engaging in unfair labor practices within the meaning of section 8(b), subsection(s) (list subsections) _____ of the National Labor Relations Act, and these unfair labor practices are unfair practices affecting commerce within the meaning of the Act.

2. Basis of the Charge (set forth a clear and concise statement of the facts constituting the alleged unfair labor practices)

3. Name of Employer

4. Telephone No.

5. Location of plant involved (street, city, state and ZIP code)

6. Employer representative to contact

7. Type of establishment (factory, mine, wholesaler, etc.)

8. Identify principal product or service

9. Number of workers employed

10. Full name of party filing charge

11. Address of party filing charge (street, city, state and ZIP code)

12. Telephone No.

13. DECLARATION

I declare that I have read the above charge and that the statements therein are true to the best of my knowledge and belief.

By _____

(signature of representative or person making charge)

(title or office, if any)

Address _____

(Telephone No.)   (date)

WILLFUL FALSE STATEMENTS ON THIS CHARGE CAN BE PUNISHED BY FINE AND IMPRISONMENT (U. S. CODE, TITLE 18, SECTION 1001)

*U.S. GPO: 2000-464-640/29074

APPENDIX 12:
NLRB CHARGE WITHDRAWAL REQUEST

PLEASE REVIEW THE FOLLOWING
IMPORTANT INFORMATION
BEFORE FILLING OUT A WITHDRAWAL REQUEST

- Please call the Board Agent to whom your pending petition or charge is assigned for assistance in filing a withdrawal request. The Board Agent will be happy to answer your questions about the withdrawal request form or to draft the withdrawal request form on your behalf. Seeking assistance from the Board Agent to whom your charge or petition is assigned may help you to avoid having the processing of your withdrawal request delayed or having your charge or petition dismissed because of mistakes made in completing the form.

- Please enter the complete case name(s) and assigned case number(s) of the charge(s) or petition(s) for which the withdrawal request is being submitted.

- After completing the withdrawal request form, be sure to sign and date the withdrawal request and mail, fax or hand deliver the completed form to the appropriate Regional Office.

- A withdrawal of the charge or petition is not automatic upon the filing of the form. The Regional Director must approve the withdrawal request. Generally, you should orally inform the Board Agent to whom your case is assigned that you intend to file such a request and the date you will send it to the Regional Office. If a withdrawal request is not received within the time period communicated to the Board Agent to whom your charge or petition is assigned, the Board Agent may recommend that the charge be dismissed.

FORM NLRB-601
(7-57)

UNITED STATES OF AMERICA
NATIONAL LABOR RELATIONS BOARD

WITHDRAWAL REQUEST

In the matter of ....
(Name of case)   (Number of case)

This is to request withdrawal of the *(petition)* *(charge)* in the above case.

....
(Name of Party Filing)

Withdrawal request approved

By ....
(Name of Representative)

....
(Date)

....
(Title)

....
Regional Director,
National Labor Relations Board.

Date ....

*U.S. GPO: 2000-464-641/29073

APPENDIX 13:
NLRB REVIEW REQUEST WAIVER FORM

PLEASE REVIEW THE FOLLOWING
IMPORTANT INFORMATION
BEFORE FILLING OUT A WAIVER TO REQUEST REVIEW FORM!

- Please call the Board Agent to whom the petition is assigned for assistance in filing a waiver of the right to request review of or file exceptions to the Regional Director's and/or Hearing Officer's representation decision and/or report. The Board Agent will be happy to answer your questions about the waiver to request review form or to draft the waiver on your behalf. Seeking assistance from the Board Agent to whom the petition is assigned may help you to avoid having the processing of your waiver delayed because of mistakes made in completing the form.

- Please state the complete case name and assigned case number of the petition for which the decision and/or report was issued and for which the waiver of the right to request review is being submitted.

- Be sure to identify the decision and/or report for which the waiver of the right to request review is being submitted, as well as, to state the date of the document or check the appropriate box if the document has not issued when the waiver of request form is completed.

- After completing the waiver of the right to request review form, be sure to sign and date the waiver and mail, fax or hand deliver the completed form to the appropriate Regional Office.

FORM NLRB-4480
(5-84)

UNITED STATES OF AMERICA
NATIONAL LABOR RELATIONS BOARD

WAIVER

IN THE MATTER OF _____   _____

(Name of Case)   (Number of Case)

PURSUANT TO SECTION 102.67 AND 102.69 OF THE RULES AND REGULATIONS OF THE NATIONAL LABOR RELATIONS BOARD,
THE UNDERSIGNED PARTY WAIVES ITS RIGHT TO REQUEST REVIEW OF OR FILE EXCEPTIONS TO THE REGIONAL DIRECTOR'S
AND/OR HEARING OFFICER'S

_____ IN THE ABOVE-

(Name of document or applicable documents)

CAPTIONED MATTER. _____ OR ☐ CHECK IF DOCUMENT NOT YET ISSUED.

(Date of document)

_____

(Name of Party)

BY _____

(Name of Representative)

_____

(Title)

DATE _____

APPENDIX 14:
SELECTED PROVISIONS OF THE CIVIL SERVICE REFORM ACT—Title 5, Chapter 71, United States Code

SUBCHAPTER I—GENERAL PROVISIONS

§ 7101. Findings and purpose

(a) The Congress finds that—

(1) experience in both private and public employment indicates that the statutory protection of the right of employees to organize, bargain collectively, and participate through labor organizations of their own choosing in decisions which affect them—

(A) safeguards the public interest,

(B) contributes to the effective conduct of public business, and

(C) facilitates and encourages the amicable settlements of disputes between employees and their employers involving conditions of employment; and

(2) the public interest demands the highest standards of employee performance and the continued development and implementation of modern and progressive work practices to facilitate and improve employee performance and the efficient accomplishment of the operations of the Government. Therefore, labor organizations and collective bargaining in the civil service are in the public interest.

(b) It is the purpose of this chapter to prescribe certain rights and obligations of the employees of the Federal Government and to establish procedures which are designed to meet the special requirements and needs of the Government. The provisions of this chapter should be interpreted in a manner consistent with the requirement of an effective and efficient Government.

§ 7102. Employees' rights

Each employee shall have the right to form, join, or assist any labor organization, or to refrain from any such activity, freely and without fear of penalty or reprisal, and each employee shall be protected in the exercise of such right. Except as otherwise provided under this chapter, such right includes the right—

(1) to act for a labor organization in the capacity of a representative and the right, in that capacity, to present the views of the labor organization to heads of agencies and other officials of the executive branch of the Government, the Congress, or other appropriate authorities, and

(2) to engage in collective bargaining with respect to conditions of employment through representatives chosen by employees under this chapter.

§ 7104. Federal Labor Relations Authority

(a) The Federal Labor Relations Authority is composed of three members, not more than 2 of whom may be adherents of the same political party. No member shall engage in any other business or employment or hold another office or position in the Government of the United States except as otherwise provided by law.

(b) Members of the Authority shall be appointed by the President by and with the advice and consent of the Senate, and may be removed by the President only upon notice and hearing and only for inefficiency, neglect of duty, or malfeasance in office. The President shall designate one member to serve as Chairman of the Authority. The Chairman is the chief executive and administrative officer of the Authority.

(c) A member of the Authority shall be appointed for a term of 5 years. An individual chosen to fill a vacancy shall be appointed for the unexpired term of the member replaced. The term of any member shall not expire before the earlier of—

(1) the date on which the member's successor takes office, or

(2) the last day of the Congress beginning after the date on which the member's term of office would (but for this paragraph) expire.

(d) A vacancy in the Authority shall not impair the right of the remaining members to exercise all of the powers of the Authority.

(e) The Authority shall make an annual report to the President for transmittal to the Congress which shall include information as to the cases it has heard and decisions it has rendered.

(f)(1) The General Counsel of the Authority shall be appointed by the President, by and with the advice and consent of the Senate, for a term of 5 years. The General Counsel may be removed at any time by the President. The General Counsel shall hold no other office or position in the Government of the United States except as provided by law.

(2) The General Counsel may—

(A) investigate alleged unfair labor practices under this chapter,

(B) file and prosecute complaints under this chapter, and

(C) exercise such other powers of the Authority as the Authority may prescribe.

(3) The General Counsel shall have direct authority over, and responsibility for, all employees in the office of General Counsel, including employees of the General Counsel in the regional offices of the Authority.

§ 7105. Powers and duties of the Authority

(a)(1) The Authority shall provide leadership in establishing policies and guidance relating to matters under this chapter, and, except as otherwise provided, shall be responsible for carrying out the purpose of this chapter.

(2) The Authority shall, to the extent provided in this chapter and in accordance with regulations prescribed by the Authority—

(A) determine the appropriateness of units for labor organization representation under section 7112 of this title;

(B) supervise or conduct elections to determine whether a labor organization has been selected as an exclusive representative by a majority of the employees in an appropriate unit and otherwise administer the provisions of section 7111 of this title relating to the according of exclusive recognition to labor organizations;

(C) prescribe criteria and resolve issues relating to the granting of national consultation rights under section 7113 of this title;

(D) prescribe criteria and resolve issues relating to determining compelling need for agency rules or regulations under section 7117(b) of this title;

(E) resolve issues relating to the duty to bargain in good faith under section 7117(c) of this title;

(F) prescribe criteria relating to the granting of consultation rights with respect to conditions of employment under section 7117(d) of this title;

(G) conduct hearings and resolve complaints of unfair labor practices under section 7118 of this title;

(H) resolve exceptions to arbitrator's awards under section 7122 of this title; and

(I) take such other actions as are necessary and appropriate to effectively administer the provisions of this chapter.

(b) The Authority shall adopt an official seal which shall be judicially noticed.

(c) The principal office of the Authority shall be in or about the District of Columbia, but the Authority may meet and exercise any or all of its powers at any time or place. Except as otherwise expressly provided by law, the Authority may, by one or more of its members or by such agents as it may designate, make any appropriate inquiry necessary to carry out its duties wherever persons subject to this chapter are located. Any member who participates in the inquiry shall not be disqualified from later participating in a decision of the Authority in any case relating to the inquiry.

(d) The Authority shall appoint an Executive Director and such regional directors, administrative law judges under section 3105 of this title, and other individuals as it may from time to time find necessary for the proper performance of its functions. The Authority may delegate to officers and employees appointed under this subsection authority to perform such duties and make such expenditures as may be necessary.

(e)(1) The Authority may delegate to any regional director its authority under this chapter—

(A) to determine whether a group of employees is an appropriate unit;

(B) to conduct investigations and to provide for hearings;

(C) to determine whether a question of representation exists and to direct an election; and

(D) to supervise or conduct secret ballot elections and certify the results thereof.

(2) The Authority may delegate to any administrative law judge appointed under subsection (d) of this section its authority under section 7118 of this title to determine whether any person has engaged in or is engaging in an unfair labor practice.

(f) If the Authority delegates any authority to any regional director or administrative law judge to take any action pursuant to subsection (e) of this section, the Authority may, upon application by any interested person filed within 60 days after the date of the action, review such action, but the review shall not, unless specifically ordered by the Authority, operate as a stay of action. The Authority may affirm, modify, or reverse any action reviewed under this subsection. If the Authority does not undertake to grant review of the action under this subsection within 60 days after the later of—

(1) the date of the action; or

(2) the date of the filing of any application under this subsection for review of the action; the action shall become the action of the Authority at the end of such 60-day period.

(g) In order to carry out its functions under this chapter, the Authority may—

(1) hold hearings;

(2) administer oaths, take the testimony or deposition of any person under oath, and issue subpenas as provided in section 7132 of this title; and

(3) may require an agency or a labor organization to cease and desist from violations of this chapter and require it to take any remedial action it considers appropriate to carry out the policies of this chapter.

(h) Except as provided in section 518 of title 28, relating to litigation before the Supreme Court, attorneys designated by the Authority may appear for the Authority and represent the Authority in any civil action brought in connection with any function carried out by the Authority pursuant to this title or as otherwise authorized by law.

(i) In the exercise of the functions of the Authority under this title, the Authority may request from the Director of the Office of Personnel Management an advisory opinion concerning the proper interpretation of rules, regulations, or policy directives issued by the Office of Personnel Management in connection with any matter before the Authority.

§ 7106. Management rights

(a) Subject to subsection (b) of this section, nothing in this chapter shall affect the authority of any management official of any agency—

(1) to determine the mission, budget, organization, number of employees, and internal security practices of the agency; and

(2) in accordance with applicable laws—

(A) to hire, assign, direct, layoff, and retain employees in the agency, or to suspend, remove, reduce in grade or pay, or take other disciplinary action against such employees;

(B) to assign work, to make determinations with respect to contracting out, and to determine the personnel by which agency operations shall be conducted;

(C) with respect to filling positions, to make selections for appointments from—

(i) among properly ranked and certified candidates for promotion; or

(ii) any other appropriate source; and

(D) to take whatever actions may be necessary to carry out the agency mission during emergencies.

(b) Nothing in this section shall preclude any agency and any labor organization from negotiating—

(1) at the election of the agency, on the numbers, types, and grades of employees or positions assigned to any organizational subdivision, work project, or tour of duty, or on the technology, methods, and means of performing work;

(2) procedures which management officials of the agency will observe in exercising any authority under this section; or

(3) appropriate arrangements for employees adversely affected by the exercise of any authority under this section by such management officials.

SUBCHAPTER II—RIGHTS AND DUTIES OF AGENCIES AND LABOR ORGANIZATIONS

§ 7111. Exclusive recognition of labor organizations

(a) An agency shall accord exclusive recognition to a labor organization if the organization has been selected as the representative, in a secret ballot election, by a majority of the employees in an appropriate unit who cast valid ballots in the election.

(b) If a petition is filed with the Authority—

(1) by any person alleging—

(A) in the case of an appropriate unit for which there is no exclusive representative, that 30 percent of the employees in the appropriate unit wish to be represented for the purpose of collective bargaining by an exclusive representative, or

(B) in the case of an appropriate unit for which there is an exclusive representative, that 30 percent of the employees in the unit allege that the exclusive representative is no longer the representative of the majority of the employees in the unit; or

(2) by any person seeking clarification of, or an amendment to, a certification then in effect or a matter relating to representation; the Authority shall investigate the petition, and if it has reasonable cause to believe that a question of representation exists, it shall provide an opportunity for a hearing (for which a transcript shall be kept) after a reasonable notice. If the Authority finds on the record of the hearing that a question of representation exists, the Authority shall supervise or conduct an election on the question by secret ballot and shall certify the results thereof. An election under this subsection shall not be conducted in any appropriate unit or in any subdivision thereof within which, in the preceding 12 calendar months, a valid election under this subsection has been held.

(c) A labor organization which—

(1) has been designated by at least 10 percent of the employees in the unit specified in any petition filed pursuant to subsection (b) of this section;

(2) has submitted a valid copy of a current or recently expired collective bargaining agreement for the unit; or

(3) has submitted other evidence that it is the exclusive representative of the employees involved; may intervene with respect to a petition filed pursuant to subsection (b) of this section and shall be placed on the ballot of any election under such subsection (b) with respect to the petition.

(d) The Authority shall determine who is eligible to vote in any election under this section and shall establish rules governing any such election, which shall include rules allowing employees eligible to vote the opportunity to choose—

(1) from labor organizations on the ballot, that labor organization which the employees wish to have represent them; or

(2) not to be represented by a labor organization. In any election in which no choice on the ballot receives a majority of the votes cast, a runoff election shall be conducted between the two choices receiving the highest number of votes. A labor organization which receives the majority of the votes cast in an election shall be certified by the Authority as the exclusive representative.

(e) A labor organization seeking exclusive recognition shall submit to the Authority and the agency involved a roster of its officers and representatives, a copy of its constitution and bylaws, and a statement of its objectives.

(f) Exclusive recognition shall not be accorded to a labor organization—

(1) if the Authority determines that the labor organization is subject to corrupt influences or influences opposed to democratic principles;

(2) in the case of a petition filed pursuant to subsection (b)(1)(A) of this section, if there is not credible evidence that at least 30 percent of the employees in the unit specified in the petition wish to be represented for the purpose of collective bargaining by the labor organization seeking exclusive recognition;

(3) if there is then in effect a lawful written collective bargaining agreement between the agency involved and an exclusive representative (other than the labor organization seeking exclusive recognition) covering any employees included in the unit specified in the petition, unless—

(A) the collective bargaining agreement has been in effect for more than 3 years, or

(B) the petition for exclusive recognition is filed not more than 105 days and not less than 60 days before the expiration date of the collective bargaining agreement; or

(4) if the Authority has, within the previous 12 calendar months, conducted a secret ballot election for the unit described in any petition under this section and in such election a majority of the employees voting chose a labor organization for certification as the unit's exclusive representative.

(g) Nothing in this section shall be construed to prohibit the waiving of hearings by stipulation for the purpose of a consent election in conformity with regulations and rules or decisions of the Authority.

§ 7112. Determination of appropriate units for labor organization representation

(a) The Authority shall determine the appropriateness of any unit. The Authority shall determine in each case whether, in order to ensure employees the fullest freedom in exercising the rights guaranteed under this chapter, the appropriate unit should be established on an agency, plant, installation, functional, or other basis and shall determine any unit to be an appropriate unit only if the determination will ensure a clear and identifiable community of interest among the employees in the unit and will promote effective dealings with, and efficiency of the operations of the agency involved.

(b) A unit shall not be determined to be appropriate under this section solely on the basis of the extent to which employees in the proposed unit have organized, nor shall a unit be determined to be appropriate if it includes—

(1) except as provided under section 7135(a)(2) of this title, any management official or supervisor;

(2) a confidential employee;

(3) an employee engaged in personnel work in other than a purely clerical capacity;

(4) an employee engaged in administering the provisions of this chapter;

(5) both professional employees and other employees, unless a majority of the professional employees vote for inclusion in the unit;

(6) any employee engaged in intelligence, counterintelligence, investigative, or security work which directly affects national security; or

(7) any employee primarily engaged in investigation or audit functions relating to the work of individuals employed by an agency whose duties directly affect the internal security of the agency, but only if the functions are undertaken to ensure that the duties are discharged honestly and with integrity.

(c) Any employee who is engaged in administering any provision of law relating to labor-management relations may not be represented by a labor organization—

(1) which represents other individuals to whom such provision applies; or

(2) which is affiliated directly or indirectly with an organization which represents other individuals to whom such provision applies.

(d) Two or more units which are in an agency and for which a labor organization is the exclusive representative may, upon petition by the agency or labor organization, be consolidated with or without an election into a single larger unit if the Authority considers the larger unit to be appropriate. The Authority shall certify the labor organization as the exclusive representative of the new larger unit.

§ 7113. National consultation rights

(a) If, in connection with any agency, no labor organization has been accorded exclusive recognition on an agency basis, a labor organization which is the exclusive representative of a substantial number of the employees of the agency, as determined in accordance with criteria prescribed by the Authority, shall be granted national consultation rights by the agency. National consultation rights shall terminate when the labor organization no longer meets the criteria prescribed by the Authority. Any issue relating to any labor organization's eligibility for, or continuation of, national consultation rights shall be subject to determination by the Authority.

(b)(1) Any labor organization having national consultation rights in connection with any agency under subsection (a) of this section shall—

(A) be informed of any substantive change in conditions of employment proposed by the agency, and

(B) be permitted reasonable time to present its views and recommendations regarding the changes.

(2) If any views or recommendations are presented under paragraph (1) of this subsection to an agency by any labor organization—

(A) the agency shall consider the views or recommendations before taking final action on any matter with respect to which the views or recommendations are presented; and

(B) the agency shall provide the labor organization a written statement of the reasons for taking the final action.

(c) Nothing in this section shall be construed to limit the right of any agency or exclusive representative to engage in collective bargaining.

§ 7114. Representation rights and duties

(a)(1) A labor organization which has been accorded exclusive recognition is the exclusive representative of the employees in the unit it represents and is entitled to act for, and negotiate collective bargaining agreements covering, all employees in the unit. An exclusive representative is responsible for representing the interests of all employees in the unit it represents without discrimination and without regard to labor organization membership.

(2) An exclusive representative of an appropriate unit in an agency shall be given the opportunity to be represented at—

(A) any formal discussion between one or more representatives of the agency and one or more employees in the unit or their representatives concerning any grievance or any personnel policy or practices or other general condition of employment; or

(B) any examination of an employee in the unit by a representative of the agency in connection with an investigation if—

(i) the employee reasonably believes that the examination may result in disciplinary action against the employee; and

(ii) the employee requests representation.

(3) Each agency shall annually inform its employees of their rights under paragraph (2)(B) of this subsection.

(4) Any agency and any exclusive representative in any appropriate unit in the agency, through appropriate representatives, shall meet and negotiate in good faith for the purposes of arriving at a collective bargaining agreement. In addition, the agency and the exclusive representative may determine appropriate techniques, consistent with the provisions of section 7119 of this title, to assist in any negotiation.

(5) The rights of an exclusive representative under the provisions of this subsection shall not be construed to preclude an employee from—

(A) being represented by an attorney or other representative, other than the exclusive representative, of the employee's own choosing in any grievance or appeal action; or

(B) exercising grievance or appellate rights established by law, rule, or regulation; except in the case of grievance or appeal procedures negotiated under this chapter.

(b) The duty of an agency and an exclusive representative to negotiate in good faith under subsection (a) of this section shall include the obligation—

(1) to approach the negotiations with a sincere resolve to reach a collective bargaining agreement;

(2) to be represented at the negotiations by duly authorized representatives prepared to discuss and negotiate on any condition of employment;

(3) to meet at reasonable times and convenient places as frequently as may be necessary, and to avoid unnecessary delays;

(4) in the case of an agency, to furnish to the exclusive representative involved, or its authorized representative, upon request and, to the extent not prohibited by law, data—

(A) which is normally maintained by the agency in the regular course of business;

(B) which is reasonably available and necessary for full and proper discussion, understanding, and negotiation of subjects within the scope of collective bargaining; and

(C) which does not constitute guidance, advice, counsel, or training provided for management officials or supervisors, relating to collective bargaining; and

(5) if agreement is reached, to execute on the request of any party to the negotiation a written document embodying the agreed terms, and to take such steps as are necessary to implement such agreement.

(c)(1) An agreement between any agency and an exclusive representative shall be subject to approval by the head of the agency.

(2) The head of the agency shall approve the agreement within 30 days from the date the agreement is executed if the agreement is in accordance with the provisions of this chapter and any other applicable law, rule, or regulation (unless the agency has granted an exception to the provision).

(3) If the head of the agency does not approve or disapprove the agreement within the 30-day period, the agreement shall take effect and shall be binding on the agency and the exclusive representative subject to the provisions of this chapter and any other applicable law, rule, or regulation.

(4) A local agreement subject to a national or other controlling agreement at a higher level shall be approved under the procedures of the controlling agreement or, if none, under regulations prescribed by the agency.

§ 7116. Unfair labor practices

(a) For the purpose of this chapter, it shall be an unfair labor practice for an agency—

(1) to interfere with, restrain, or coerce any employee in the exercise by the employee of any right under this chapter;

(2) to encourage or discourage membership in any labor organization by discrimination in connection with hiring, tenure, promotion, or other conditions of employment;

(3) to sponsor, control, or otherwise assist any labor organization, other than to furnish, upon request, customary and routine services and facilities if the services and facilities are also furnished on an impartial basis to other labor organizations having equivalent status;

(4) to discipline or otherwise discriminate against an employee because the employee has filed a complaint, affidavit, or petition, or has given any information or testimony under this chapter;

(5) to refuse to consult or negotiate in good faith with a labor organization as required by this chapter;

(6) to fail or refuse to cooperate in impasse procedures and impasse decisions as required by this chapter;

(7) to enforce any rule or regulation (other than a rule or regulation implementing section 2302 of this title) which is in conflict with any applicable collective bargaining agreement if the agreement was in effect before the date the rule or regulation was prescribed; or

(8) to otherwise fail or refuse to comply with any provision of this chapter.

(b) For the purpose of this chapter, it shall be an unfair labor practice for a labor organization—

(1) to interfere with, restrain, or coerce any employee in the exercise by the employee of any right under this chapter;

(2) to cause or attempt to cause an agency to discriminate against any employee in the exercise by the employee of any right under this chapter;

(3) to coerce, discipline, fine, or attempt to coerce a member of the labor organization as punishment, reprisal, or for the purpose of hindering or impeding the member's work performance or productivity as an employee or the discharge of the member's duties as an employee;

(4) to discriminate against an employee with regard to the terms or conditions of membership in the labor organization on the basis of race, color, creed, national origin, sex, age, preferential or nonpreferential civil service status, political affiliation, marital status, or handicapping condition;

(5) to refuse to consult or negotiate in good faith with an agency as required by this chapter;

(6) to fail or refuse to cooperate in impasse procedures and impasse decisions as required by this chapter;

(7)(A) to call, or participate in, a strike, work stoppage, or slowdown, or picketing of an agency in a labor-management dispute if such picketing interferes with an agency's operations, or

(B) to condone any activity described in subparagraph (A) of this paragraph by failing to take action to prevent or stop such activity; or

(8) to otherwise fail or refuse to comply with any provision of this chapter.

Nothing in paragraph (7) of this subsection shall result in any informational picketing which does not interfere with an agency's operations being considered as an unfair labor practice.

(c) For the purpose of this chapter it shall be an unfair labor practice for an exclusive representative to deny membership to any employee in the appropriate unit represented by such exclusive representative except for failure—

(1) to meet reasonable occupational standards uniformly required for admission, or

(2) to tender dues uniformly required as a condition of acquiring and retaining membership.

This subsection does not preclude any labor organization from enforcing discipline in accordance with procedures under its constitution or bylaws to the extent consistent with the provisions of this chapter.

(d) Issues which can properly be raised under an appeals procedure may not be raised as unfair labor practices prohibited under this section. Except for matters wherein, under section 7121(e) and (f) of this title, an employee has an option of using the negotiated grievance procedure or an appeals procedure, issues which can be raised under a grievance procedure may, in the discretion of the aggrieved party, be raised under the grievance procedure or as an unfair labor practice under this section, but not under both procedures.

(e) The expression of any personal view, argument, opinion or the making of any statement which—

(1) publicizes the fact of a representational election and encourages employees to exercise their right to vote in such election,

(2) corrects the record with respect to any false or misleading statement made by any person, or

(3) informs employees of the Government's policy relating to labor-management relations and representation, shall not, if the expression contains no threat or reprisal or force or promise of benefit or was not made under coercive conditions, (A) constitute an unfair labor practice under any provision of this chapter, or (B) constitute grounds for the setting aside of any election conducted under any provisions of this chapter.

§ 7117. Duty to bargain in good faith; compelling need; duty to consult

(a)(1) Subject to paragraph (2) of this subsection, the duty to bargain in good faith shall, to the extent not inconsistent with any Federal law or any Government-wide rule or regulation, extend to matters which are the subject of any rule or regulation only if the rule or regulation is not a Government-wide rule or regulation.

(2) The duty to bargain in good faith shall, to the extent not inconsistent with Federal law or any Government-wide rule or regulation, extend to matters which are the subject of any agency rule or regulation referred to in paragraph (3) of this subsection only if the Authority has determined under subsection (b) of this section that no compelling need (as determined under regulations prescribed by the Authority) exists for the rule or regulation.

(3) Paragraph (2) of the subsection applies to any rule or regulation issued by any agency or issued by any primary national subdivision of such agency, unless an exclusive representative represents an appropriate unit including not less than a majority of the employees in the issuing agency or primary national subdivision, as the case may be, to whom the rule or regulation is applicable.

(b)(1) In any case of collective bargaining in which an exclusive representative alleges that no compelling need exists for any rule or regulation referred to in subsection (a)(3) of this section which is then in effect and which governs any matter at issue in such collective bargaining, the Authority shall determine under paragraph (2) of this subsection, in accordance with regulations prescribed by the Authority, whether such a compelling need exists.

(2) For the purpose of this section, a compelling need shall be determined not to exist for any rule or regulation only if—

(A) the agency, or primary national subdivision, as the case may be, which issued the rule or regulation informs the Authority in writing that a compelling need for the rule or regulation does not exist; or

(B) the Authority determines that a compelling need for a rule or regulation does not exist.

(3) A hearing may be held, in the discretion of the Authority, before a determination is made under this subsection. If a hearing is held, it shall be expedited to the extent practicable and shall not include the General Counsel as a party.

(4) The agency, or primary national subdivision, as the case may be, which issued the rule or regulation shall be a necessary party at any hearing under this subsection.

(c)(1) Except in any case to which subsection (b) of this section applies, if an agency involved in collective bargaining with an exclusive representative alleges that the duty to bargain in good faith does not extend to any matter, the exclusive representative may appeal the allegation to the Authority in accordance with the provisions of this subsection.

(2) The exclusive representative may, on or before the 15th day after the date on which the agency first makes the allegation referred to in paragraph (1) of this subsection, institute an appeal under this subsection by—

(A) filing a petition with the Authority; and

(B) furnishing a copy of the petition to the head of the agency.

(3) On or before the 30th day after the date of the receipt by the head of the agency of the copy of the petition under paragraph (2)(B) of this subsection, the agency shall—

(A) file with the Authority a statement—

(i) withdrawing the allegation; or

(ii) setting forth in full its reasons supporting the allegation; and

(B) furnish a copy of such statement to the exclusive representative.

(4) On or before the 15th day after the date of the receipt by the exclusive representative of a copy of a statement under paragraph (3)(B) of this subsection, the exclusive representative shall file with the Authority its response to the statement.

(5) A hearing may be held, in the discretion of the Authority, before a determination is made under this subsection. If a hearing is held, it shall not include the General Counsel as a party.

(6) The Authority shall expedite proceedings under this subsection to the extent practicable and shall issue to the exclusive representative and to the agency a written decision on the allegation and specific reasons therefor at the earliest practicable date.

(d)(1) A labor organization which is the exclusive representative of a substantial number of employees, determined in accordance with criteria prescribed by the Authority, shall be granted consultation rights by any agency with respect to any Government-wide rule or regulation issued by the agency effecting any substantive change in any condition of employment. Such consultation rights shall terminate when the labor organization no longer meets the criteria prescribed by the Authority. Any issue relating to a labor organization's eligibility for, or continuation of, such consultation rights shall be subject to determination by the Authority.

(2) A labor organization having consultation rights under paragraph (1) of this subsection shall—

(A) be informed of any substantive change in conditions of employment proposed by the agency, and

(B) shall be permitted reasonable time to present its views and recommendations regarding the changes.

(3) If any views or recommendations are presented under paragraph (2) of this subsection to an agency by any labor organization—

(A) the agency shall consider the views or recommendations before taking final action on any matter with respect to which the views or recommendations are presented; and

(B) the agency shall provide the labor organization a written statement of the reasons for taking the final action.

§ 7118. Prevention of unfair labor practices

(a)(1) If any agency or labor organization is charged by any person with having engaged in or engaging in an unfair labor practice, the General Counsel shall investigate the charge and may issue and cause to be served upon the agency or labor organization a complaint. In any case in which the General Counsel does not issue a complaint because the charge fails to state an unfair labor practice, the General Counsel shall provide the person making the charge a written statement of the reasons for not issuing a complaint.

(2) Any complaint under paragraph (1) of this subsection shall contain a notice—

(A) of the charge;

(B) that a hearing will be held before the Authority (or any member thereof or before an individual employed by the authority and designated for such purpose); and

(C) of the time and place fixed for the hearing.

(3) The labor organization or agency involved shall have the right to file an answer to the original and any amended complaint and to appear in person or otherwise and give testimony at the time and place fixed in the complaint for the hearing.

(4)(A) Except as provided in subparagraph (B) of this paragraph, no complaint shall be issued on any alleged unfair labor practice which occurred more than 6 months before the filing of the charge with the Authority.

(B) If the General Counsel determines that the person filing any charge was prevented from filing the charge during the 6-month period referred to in subparagraph (A) of this paragraph by reason of—

(i) any failure of the agency or labor organization against which the charge is made to perform a duty owed to the person, or

(ii) any concealment which prevented discovery of the alleged unfair labor practice during the 6- month period, the General Counsel may issue a complaint based on the charge if the charge was filed during the 6-month period beginning on the day of the discovery by the person of the alleged unfair labor practice.

(5) The General Counsel may prescribe regulations providing for informal methods by which the alleged unfair labor practice may be resolved prior to the issuance of a complaint.

(6) The Authority (or any member thereof or any individual employed by the Authority and designated for such purpose) shall conduct a hearing on the complaint not earlier than 5 days after the date on which the complaint is served. In the discretion of the individual or individuals conducting the hearing, any person involved may be allowed to intervene in the hearing and to present testimony. Any such hearing shall, to the extent practicable, be conducted in accordance with the provisions of subchapter II of chapter 5 of this title, except that the parties shall not be bound by rules of evidence, whether statutory, common law, or adopted by a court. A transcript shall be kept of the hearing. After such a hearing the Authority, in its discretion, may upon notice receive further evidence or hear argument.

(7) If the Authority (or any member thereof or any individual employed by the Authority and designated for such purpose) determines after any hearing on a complaint under paragraph (5) of this subsection that the preponderance of the evidence received demonstrates that the agency or labor organization named in the complaint has engaged in or is engaging in an unfair labor practice, then the individual or individuals conducting the hearing shall state in writing their findings of fact and shall issue and cause to be served on the agency or labor organization an order—

(A) to cease and desist from any such unfair labor practice in which the agency or labor organization is engaged;

(B) requiring the parties to renegotiate a collective bargaining agreement in accordance with the order of the Authority and requiring that the agreement, as amended, be given retroactive effect;

(C) requiring reinstatement of an employee with backpay in accordance with section 5596 of this title; or

(D) including any combination of the actions described in subparagraphs (A) through (C) of this paragraph or such other action as will carry out the purpose of this chapter. If any such order requires reinstatement of any employee with backpay, backpay may be required of the agency (as provided in section 5596 of this title) or of the labor organization, as the case may be, which is found to have engaged in the unfair labor practice involved.

(8) If the individual or individuals conducting the hearing determine that the preponderance of the evidence received fails to demonstrate that the agency or labor organization named in the complaint has engaged in or is engaging in an unfair labor practice, the individual or individuals shall state in writing their findings of fact and shall issue an order dismissing the complaint.

(b) In connection with any matter before the Authority in any proceeding under this section, the Authority may request, in accordance with the provisions of section 7105(i) of this title, from the Director of the Office of Personnel Management an advisory opinion concerning the proper interpretation of rules, regulations, or other policy directives issued by the Office of Personnel Management.

§ 7119. Negotiation impasses; Federal Service Impasses Panel

(a) The Federal Mediation and Conciliation Service shall provide services and assistance to agencies and exclusive representatives in the resolution of negotiation impasses. The Service shall determine under what circumstances and in what matter it shall provide services and assistance.

(b) If voluntary arrangements, including the services of the Federal Mediation and Conciliation Service or any other third-party mediation, fail to resolve a negotiation impasse—

(1) either party may request the Federal Service Impasses Panel to consider the matter, or

(2) the parties may agree to adopt a procedure for binding arbitration of the negotiation impasses, but only if the procedure is approved by the Panel.

(c)(1) The Federal Service Impasses Panel is an entity within the Authority, the function of which is to provide assistance in resolving negotiation impasses between agencies and exclusive representatives.

(2) The Panel shall be composed of a Chairman and at least six other members, who shall be appointed by the President, solely on the basis of fitness to perform duties and functions involved, from among individuals who are familiar with Government operations and knowledgeable in labor-management relations.

(3) Of the original members of the Panel, 2 members shall be appointed for a term of 1 year, 2 members shall be appointed for a term of 3 years, and the Chairman and the remaining members shall be appointed for a term of 5 years. Thereafter each member shall be appointed for a term of 5 years, except that an individual chosen to fill a vacancy shall be appointed for the unexpired term of the member replaced. Any member of the Panel may be removed by the President.

(4) The Panel may appoint an Executive Director and any other individuals it may from time to time find necessary for the proper performance of its duties. Each member of the Panel who is not an employee (as defined in section 2105 of this title) is entitled to pay at a rate equal to the daily equivalent of the maximum annual rate of basic pay then currently paid under the General Schedule for each day he is engaged in the performance of official business of the Panel, including travel time, and is entitled to travel expenses as provided under section 5703 of this title.

(5)(A) The Panel or its designee shall promptly investigate any impasse presented to it under subsection (b) of this section. The Panel shall consider the impasse and shall either—

(i) recommend to the parties procedures for the resolution of the impasse; or

(ii) assist the parties in resolving the impasse through whatever methods and procedures, including factfinding and recommendations, it may consider appropriate to accomplish the purpose of this section.

(B) If the parties do not arrive at a settlement after assistance by the Panel under subparagraph (A) of this paragraph, the Panel may—

(i) hold hearings;

(ii) administer oaths, take the testimony or deposition of any person under oath, and issue subpenas as provided in section 7132 of this title; and

(iii) take whatever action is necessary and not inconsistent with this chapter to resolve the impasse.

(C) Notice of any final action of the Panel under this section shall be promptly served upon the parties, and the action shall be binding on such parties during the term of the agreement, unless the parties agree otherwise.

§ 7120. Standards of conduct for labor organizations

(a) An agency shall only accord recognition to a labor organization that is free from corrupt influences and influences opposed to basic democratic principles. Except as provided in subsection (b) of this section, an organization is not required to prove that it is free from such influences if it is subject to governing requirements adopted by the organization or by a national or international labor organization or federation of labor organizations with which it is affiliated, or in which it participates, containing explicit and detailed provisions to which it subscribes calling for—

(1) the maintenance of democratic procedures and practices including provisions for periodic elections to be conducted subject to recognized safeguards and provisions defining and securing the right of individual members to participate in the affairs of the organization, to receive fair and equal treatment under the governing rules of the organization, and to receive fair process in disciplinary proceedings;

(2) the exclusion from office in the organization of persons affiliated with communist or other totalitarian movements and persons identified with corrupt influences;

(3) the prohibition of business or financial interests on the part of organization officers and agents which conflict with their duty to the organization and its members; and

(4) the maintenance of fiscal integrity in the conduct of the affairs of the organization, including provisions for accounting and financial controls and regular financial reports or summaries to be made available to members.

(b) Notwithstanding the fact that a labor organization has adopted or subscribed to standards of conduct as provided in subsection (a) of this section, the organization is required to furnish evidence of its freedom from corrupt influences or influences opposed to basic democratic principles if there is reasonable cause to believe that—

(1) the organization has been suspended or expelled from, or is subject to other sanction, by a parent labor organization, or federation of organizations with which it had been affiliated, because it has demonstrated an unwillingness or inability to comply with governing requirements comparable in purpose to those required by subsection (a) of this section; or

(2) the organization is in fact subject to influences that would preclude recognition under this chapter.

(c) A labor organization which has or seeks recognition as a representative of employees under this chapter shall file financial and other reports with the Assistant Secretary of Labor for Labor Management Relations, provide for bonding of officials and employees of the organization, and comply with trusteeship and election standards.

(d) The Assistant Secretary shall prescribe such regulations as are necessary to carry out the purposes of this section. Such regulations shall conform generally to the principles applied to labor organizations in the private sector. Complaints of violations of this section shall be filed with the Assistant Secretary. In any matter arising under this section, the Assistant Secretary may require a labor organization to cease and desist from violations of this section and require it to take such actions as he considers appropriate to carry out the policies of this section.

(e) This chapter does not authorize participation in the management of a labor organization or acting as a representative of a labor organization by a management official, a supervisor, or a confidential employee, except as specifically provided in this chapter, or by an employee if the participation or activity would result in a conflict or apparent conflict of interest or would otherwise be incompatible with law or with the official duties of the employee.

(f) In the case of any labor organization which by omission or commission has willfully and intentionally, with regard to any strike, work stoppage, or slowdown, violated section 7116(b)(7) of this title, the Authority shall, upon an appropriate finding by the Authority of such violation—

(1) revoke the exclusive recognition status of the labor organization, which shall then immediately cease to be legally entitled and obligated to represent employees in the unit; or

(2) take any other appropriate disciplinary action.

APPENDIX 15:
FLRA REPRESENTATION PETITION

OMB Control No. 3070-0003
Approved through 3/31/99

UNITED STATES OF AMERICA	FOR FLRA USE ONLY
FEDERAL LABOR RELATIONS AUTHORITY	
PETITION	Case No
	Date Filed

See instructions on the back of this form. Attach additional sheets if needed, numbered according to the item to which they pertain. By signing the petition form, a labor organization/petitioner certifies it has submitted to the agency or activity and to the Department of Labor a roster of its officers and representatives, a copy of its constitution and by-laws, and a statement of its objectives.

1. Clear and concise statement of the purpose of the petition and the issues raised by the petition.

2. Description of the unit(s):

Included:

Excluded:

3. Approximate number of employees in the unit(s) affected by issues raised in the petition.

Currently _____
Proposed _____

4. The petition is supported by:

____ a showing of interest of not less than 30%
____ evidence of membership of not less than 10% of the employees in the unit(s) involved in the petition.

5. PETITIONER:

NAME	AFFILIATION / DEPARTMENT	ADDRESS (Street and Number, City, State, and ZIP Code)	PHONE NO.
A. Petitioner			
B. Petitioner Contact			

6. AGENCY(IES), OTHER THAN PETITIONER, AFFECTED BY THE PETITION:

NAME	DEPARTMENT	ADDRESS (Street and Number, City, State, and ZIP Code)	PHONE NO.
A. Activity/Agency			
B. Activity/Agency Contact			

7. LABOR ORGANIZATION(S), OTHER THAN PETITIONER, AFFECTED BY THE PETITION:

NAME	AFFILIATION	ADDRESS (Street and Number, City, State, and ZIP Code)	PHONE NO.
A. Labor Organization			
B. Labor Organization Contact			

8A. Date(s) of Recognition/Certification (Month, Day and Year) of any unit(s) affected by issues raised in the petition.

8B. Expiration of Current Agreement(s) (Month, Day and Year) covering any unit(s) affected by issues raised in the petition.

9. Name, title, address, and telephone number of person filing petition.

10. I DECLARE THAT I HAVE READ THIS PETITION AND THAT THE STATEMENTS IN IT ARE TRUE TO THE BEST OF MY KNOWLEDGE AND BELIEF. I UNDERSTAND THAT MAKING WILLFULLY FALSE STATEMENTS CAN BE PUNISHED BY FINE AND IMPRISONMENT. 18 U.S.C. 1001. THIS PETITION WAS SERVED ON ALL PARTIES KNOWN TO BE AFFECTED BY ISSUES RAISED IN THIS PETITION.

Type or Print Your Name	Your Signature	Date

FLRA Form 21(Rev. 3/96)

OVERVIEW: Use this form if you want to file a petition pursuant to Sections 7111, 7112 and 7115 of the Federal Service Labor Management Relations Statute. Refer to the Rules and Regulations of the Federal Labor Relations Authority (FLRA). Part 2422 of 5 C.F.R., for additional information on how to file a petition. An original and two (2) copies of a petition must be filed with the appropriate Regional Director, FLRA, along with a statement of any relevant facts not contained in the petition and a copy of all relevant correspondence relating to matters raised by the petition. If you do not know the address of the Regional Director, you may contact the Office of the General Counsel, FLRA, in Washington, D.C. at (202) 482-6600. Upon filing the petition, you must serve a copy of the petition and accompanying materials on all affected parties. If additional space is needed, you may attach additional sheets numbered according to the item to which they pertain. The showing of interest and alphabetical list of names constituting such showing, as required by the Statute and the FLRA's Regulations for any petition seeking an election or petition seeking a determination for dues allotment, must be filed with the petition, but may not be furnished to any other party.

PURPOSE OF THE PETITION AND STANDING TO FILE:

(A) Only a labor organization may file a petition to request: (1) an election to determine if employees in an appropriate unit wish to be represented for the purpose of collective bargaining by an exclusive representative, and/or (2) a determination of eligibility for dues allotment in an appropriate unit without an exclusive representative.

(B) Only an individual may file a petition to request an election to determine if employees in a unit no longer wish to be represented for the purpose of collective bargaining by an exclusive representative.

Petitions for the purposes described in (A) or (B) must be accompanied by a showing of interest or evidence of membership, as appropriate.

(C) An agency or a labor organization, or an agency and a labor organization jointly, may file a petition:
(1) to clarify or amend: (i) a recognition or certification then in effect (for example, to change the name or affiliation of the recognized or certified exclusive representative or the name of the agency; or to resolve questions related to the eligibility of employees for inclusion in the unit); and/or (ii) any other matter relating to representation (for example, to resolve representation questions related to a reorganization or realignment of agency operations or issues related to the majority status of the currently recognized or certified labor organization); or
(2) to consolidate two or more units, with or without an election, in an agency and for which a labor organization is the exclusive representative.

LINE BY LINE INSTRUCTIONS:

1. Provide a clear and concise statement of the purpose of the petition, the issues raised by the petition, and the results the petitioner seeks.
2. Describe the unit(s) affected by issues raised in the petition. If the petitioner is seeking an election to determine the exclusive representative of an appropriate unit of employees and/or a determination for dues allotment, the description should include the geographic location and classifications of the employees sought to be included in, or sought to be excluded from, the unit. If the petitioner is seeking an election to determine if employees no longer wish to be represented for purposes of collective bargaining by an exclusive representative or to clarify, amend or consolidate existing units, the petitioner should provide a description of the existing certification(s) or recognition(s). If more than one unit is affected, attach additional sheets.
3. State the approximate number of employees in the existing unit or the unit claimed to be appropriate; in a clarification or amendment, state the approximate number of employees in the units affected by issues raised in the petition.
4. State whether a petition seeking an election is accompanied by a showing of interest of 30% of the employees in the unit claimed to be appropriate. State whether a petition for a determination for dues allotment is accompanied by evidence of membership of 10% of the employees in the unit claimed to be appropriate.
5. Provide the name and mailing address for the petitioner and the contact person, including street and number, city, state and zip code. If a labor organization petitioner is affiliated with a national organization, provide the local designation and the national affiliation. If an activity or agency is affiliated with an executive department, provide the name of the department.
6. Provide the name and mailing address for each activity or agency other than the petitioner affected by issues raised in the petition, including street and number, city, state and zip code. Also provide the name, mailing address and work telephone number of the contact person for each activity or agency affected by issues raised in the petition. If an activity or agency is affiliated with an executive department, provide the name of the department.
7. Provide the name and mailing address for each labor organization other than the petitioner affected by issues raised in the petition, including street and number, city, state and zip code. If a labor organization is affiliated with a national organization, provide the local designation and the national affiliation. Provide the name, mailing address and work telephone number of the contact person for each labor organization affected by issues raised in the petition.
8. If the labor organization(s) named in #7 is an exclusive representative of any of the employees affected by issues raised in the petition, provide the date(s) of the recognition or certification and the date(s) any collective bargaining agreement covering the unit(s) will expire, or the most recent agreement did expire, if known.
9. State the name, title and mailing address of the person filing the petition, including street and number, city, state and zip code and telephone number .
10. Type or print the name of the person filing the petition. The person filing the petition must also sign and date the petition before it is filed.

It is estimated that it will take one hour or less to complete this form. This petition is not valid unless an OMB control number is displayed on the form.

APPENDIX 16:
FLRA UNFAIR LABOR PRACTICE CHARGE
FORM AGAINST AN AGENCY

Form Exempt Under 44 U.S.C. 3512

		FOR FLRA USE ONLY
UNITED STATES OF AMERICA **FEDERAL LABOR RELATIONS AUTHORITY** **CHARGE AGAINST AN AGENCY**	Case No.	
	Date Filed	

Complete instructions are on the back of this form.

1. Charged Activity or Agency	2. Charging Party (Labor Organization or Individual)
Name:	Name:
Address:	Address:
Tel.#: Ext.	Tel.#: Ext.
Fax#:	Fax#:

3. Charged Activity or Agency Contact Information	4. Charging Party Contact Information
Name:	Name:
Title:	Title:
Address:	Address:
Tel.#: Ext.	Tel.#: Ext.
Fax#:	Fax#:

5. Which subsection(s) of 5 U.S.C. 7116(a) do you believe have been violated? [See reverse] (1) and

6. Tell exactly WHAT the activity (or agency) did. Start with the DATE and LOCATION, state WHO was involved, including titles.

7. Have you or anyone else raised this matter in any other procedure?   No   Yes   If yes, where? [see reverse]

8. I DECLARE THAT I HAVE READ THIS CHARGE AND THAT THE STATEMENTS IN IT ARE TRUE TO THE BEST OF MY KNOWLEDGE AND BELIEF. I UNDERSTAND THAT MAKING WILLFULLY FALSE STATEMENTS CAN BE PUNISHED BY FINE AND IMPRISONMENT, 18 U.S.C. 1001. THIS CHARGE WAS SERVED ON THE PERSON IDENTIFIED IN BOX #3 BY [check "x" box]   Fax   1st Class Mail   In Person
    Commercial Delivery   Certified Mail

Type or Print Your Name	Your Signature	Date

INSTRUCTIONS FOR COMPLETING FORM 22:

<u>General</u>

Use this form if you are charging that a federal activity or agency committed an unfair labor practice under paragraph (a) of section 7116 of the Federal Service Labor-Management Relations Statute. File an original form with the appropriate Regional Director, Federal Labor Relations Authority. If you do not know that address, contact the Office of the General Counsel, Federal Labor Relations Authority, (202)482-6600. If filing the charge by fax, you need only file a fax-transmitted copy of the charge (with required signature) with the Region. You assume responsibility for receipt of a charge. A charge is a self-contained document without a need to refer to supporting evidence and documents that are also submitted to the Regional Director along with the charge. If filing a charge by fax, do **not** submit supporting evidence and documents by fax. See 5 CFR Part 2423 for an explanation of unfair labor practice proceedings and, in particular, §§ 2423.4 and 2423.6, which concern the contents, filing, and service of the charge and supporting evidence and documents.

<u>Instructions for filling out each numbered box</u>

#1. Give the full name of the activity (or agency) you are charging and the mailing address, telephone #, and fax # (if available). Include the street number, city, state, zip code. If you are charging more than one activity/agency with the same act, attach the required information on a separate sheet.

#2. Give the full name of the union or individual filing the charge and the mailing address, telephone #, and fax # (if available). If the union is affiliated with a national organization, give both the national affiliation and local designation.

#3. and **#4.** This information is essential to the investigation of your charge as it tells us who is representing the parties. Be as specific and as accurate as possible. It will assist the investigation if you include your home as well as work telephone number in the space provided.

#5. Identify which one or more of the following subsections of 5 U.S.C. 7116(a) has or have allegedly been violated. Subsection (1) has already been selected for you because a violation of (2) through (8) is an automatic violation of (1). List all sections allegedly violated:

    7116. Unfair labor practices

        (a) For the purpose of this chapter, it shall be an unfair labor practice for an agency--
        (1) to interfere with, restrain, or coerce any employee in the exercise by the employee of any right under this chapter;
        (2) to encourage or discourage membership in any labor organization by discrimination in connection with hiring, tenure, promotion, or other conditions of employment;
        (3) to sponsor, control, or otherwise assist any labor organization, other than to furnish, upon request, customary and routine services and facilities if the services and facilities are also furnished on an impartial basis to other labor organizations having equivalent status;
        (4) to discipline or otherwise discriminate against an employee because the employee has filed a complaint, affidavit, or petition, or has given any information or testimony under this chapter;
        (5) to refuse to consult or negotiate in good faith with a labor organization as required by this chapter;
        (6) to fail or refuse to cooperate in impasse procedures and impasse decisions as required by this chapter;
        (7) to enforce any rule or regulation (other than a rule or regulation implementing section 2302 of this title) which is in conflict with any applicable collective bargaining agreement if the agreement was in effect before the date the rule or regulation was prescribed; or
        (8) to otherwise fail or refuse to comply with any provision of this chapter.

#6. It is important that the basis for the charge be BRIEF, COMPLETE, and FACTUAL, rather than opinion.
    - Give dates and times of significant events as accurately as possible.
    - Give specific locations when important, e.g., "The meeting was held in the auditorium of Building 36."
    - Identify who was involved by title, e.g., "Chief Steward Pat Jones" or "Lou Smith, the File Room Supervisor."
    - Tell what happened, in chronological order.

#7. Indicate whether you or anyone else that you know of has raised this same matter in another forum:
    a. GRIEVANCE PROCEDURE
    b. FEDERAL MEDIATION AND CONCILIATION SERVICE
    c. FEDERAL SERVICE IMPASSES PANEL
    d. EQUAL EMPLOYMENT OPPORTUNITY COMMISSION
    e. MERIT SYSTEMS PROTECTION BOARD
    f. OFFICE OF SPECIAL COUNSEL
    g. OTHER ADMINISTRATIVE OR JUDICIAL PROCEEDING
    h. NEGOTIABILITY APPEAL TO FLRA

#8. Type or print your name. Then sign and date the charge attesting to the truth of the charge and that you have served the charged party (individual named in box #3). Indicate method of service by placing an "x" in one of the boxes provided.

APPENDIX 17:
FLRA UNFAIR LABOR PRACTICE CHARGE FORM AGAINST A LABOR ORGANIZATION

Form Exempt Under 44 U.S.C. 3512

UNITED STATES OF AMERICA **FEDERAL LABOR RELATIONS AUTHORITY** CHARGE AGAINST A LABOR ORGANIZATION	FOR FLRA USE ONLY
	Case No.
	Date Filed

Complete instructions are on the back of this form.

1. Charged Labor Organization	2. Charging Party (Individual, Labor Organization, Activity, or Agency)
Name:	Name:
Address:	Address:
Tel.#: Ext.	Tel.#: Ext.
Fax#:	Fax#:
3. Charged Labor Organization Contact Information	**4. Charging Party Contact Information**
Name:	Name:
Title:	Title:
Address:	Address:
Tel.#: Ext.	Tel.#: Ext.
Fax#:	Fax#:

5. Which subsection(s) of 5 U.S.C. 7116(b) and/or (c) do you believe have been violated? [See reverse] ___

6. Tell exactly WHAT the labor organization did. Start with the DATE and LOCATION, state WHO was involved, including titles.

7. Have you or anyone else raised this matter in any other procedure? ___No ___Yes   If yes, where? [see reverse]

8. I DECLARE THAT I HAVE READ THIS CHARGE AND THAT THE STATEMENTS IN IT ARE TRUE TO THE BEST OF MY KNOWLEDGE AND BELIEF. I UNDERSTAND THAT MAKING WILLFULLY FALSE STATEMENTS CAN BE PUNISHED BY FINE AND IMPRISONMENT. 18 U.S.C. 1001. THIS CHARGE WAS SERVED ON THE PERSON IDENTIFIED IN BOX #3 BY [check "x" box] ___ Fax ___ 1st Class Mail ___ In Person ___ Commercial Delivery ___ Certified Mail

Type or Print Your Name	Your Signature	Date

FLRA Form 23 (Rev. 1/99)

INSTRUCTIONS FOR COMPLETING FORM 23:

<u>General</u>

Use this form if you are charging that a labor organization or its agents committed an unfair labor practice under paragraph (b) and/or (c) of section 7116 of the Federal Service Labor-Management Relations Statute. File an original form with the appropriate Regional Director, Federal Labor Relations Authority. If you do not know that address, contact the Office of the General Counsel, Federal Labor Relations Authority, (202)482-6600. If filing the charge by fax, you need only file a fax-transmitted copy of the charge (with required signature) with the Region. You assume responsibility for receipt of a charge. A charge is a self-contained document without a need to refer to supporting evidence and documents that are also submitted to the Regional Director along with the charge. If filing a charge by fax, do **not** submit supporting evidence and documents by fax. See 5 CFR Part 2423 for an explanation of unfair labor practice proceedings and, in particular, §§ 2423.4 and 2423.6, which concern the contents, filing, and service of the charge and supporting evidence and documents.

<u>Instructions for filling out each numbered box</u>

#1. Give the full name of the labor organization (including the name of the local and number and its national or international affiliation, if any) you are charging and the mailing address, tel. #, and fax # (if available). Include the street number, city, state, zip code.

#2. Give the full name of the Charging Party and the mailing address, tel. #, and fax # (if available). If a union, and affiliated with a national organization, give both the national affiliation and local designation. If an activity, give the name of the activity, the agency, and the department of which the activity is a part. If an agency, give the name of the agency and department of which the agency is a part.

#3. and **#4.** This information is essential to the investigation of your charge as it tells us who is representing the parties. Be as specific and as accurate as possible. It will assist the investigation if you include your home as well as work telephone number in the space provided.

#5. Identify which one or more of the following subsections of 5 U.S.C. 7116(b), and/or (c) has or have allegedly been violated. List all sections allegedly violated:

(b) For the purpose of this chapter, it shall be an unfair labor practice for a labor organization--
(1) to interfere with, restrain, or coerce any employee in the exercise by the employee of any right under this chapter;
(2) to cause or attempt to cause an agency to discriminate against any employee in the exercise by the employee of any right under this chapter;
(3) to coerce, discipline, fine, or attempt to coerce a member of the labor organization as punishment, reprisal, or for the purpose of hindering or impeding the member's work performance or productivity as an employee or the discharge of the member's duties as an employee;
(4) to discriminate against an employee with regard to the terms or conditions of membership in the labor organization on the basis of race, color, creed, national origin, sex, age, preferential or nonpreferential civil service status, political affiliation, marital status, or handicapping condition;
(5) to refuse to consult or negotiate in good faith with an agency as required by this chapter;
(6) to fail or refuse to cooperate in impasse procedures and impasse decisions as required by this chapter;
(7) (A) to call, or participate in, a strike, work stoppage, or slowdown, or picketing of an agency in a labor-management dispute if such picketing interferes with an agency's operations, or
(B) to condone any activity described in subparagraph (A) of this paragraph by failing to take action to prevent or stop such activity; or
(8) to otherwise fail or refuse to comply with any provision of this chapter.

(c) For the purpose of this chapter it shall be an unfair labor practice for an exclusive representative to deny membership to any employee in the appropriate unit represented by such exclusive representative except for failure--
(1) to meet reasonable occupational standards uniformly required for admission, or
(2) to tender dues uniformly required as a condition of acquiring and retaining membership.
This subsection does not preclude any labor organization from enforcing discipline in accordance with procedures under its constitution or by laws to the extent consistent with the provisions of this chapter.

#6. It is important that the basis for the charge be BRIEF, COMPLETE, and FACTUAL, rather than opinion.
- Give dates and times of significant events as accurately as possible.
- Give specific locations when important, e.g., "The meeting was held in the auditorium of Building 36."
- Identify who was involved by title, e.g., "Chief Steward Pat Jones" or "Lou Smith, the File Room Supervisor."
- Tell what happened, in chronological order.

#7. Indicate whether you or anyone else that you know of has raised this same matter in another forum:
a. GRIEVANCE PROCEDURE
b. FEDERAL MEDIATION AND CONCILIATION SERVICE
c. FEDERAL SERVICE IMPASSES PANEL
d. EQUAL EMPLOYMENT OPPORTUNITY COMMISSION
e. MERIT SYSTEMS PROTECTION BOARD
f. OFFICE OF SPECIAL COUNSEL
g. OTHER ADMINISTRATIVE OR JUDICIAL PROCEEDING
h. NEGOTIABILITY APPEAL TO FLRA

#8. Type or print your name. Then sign and date the charge attesting to the truth of the charge and that you have served the charged party (individual named in box #3). Indicate method of service by placing an "x" in one of boxes provided.

GLOSSARY

Administrative Law Judge—As with other federal agencies (such as the Labor Department or Social Security Administration), the NLRB has a corps of judges who conduct hearings at which the parties present evidence. These judges work for the NLRB (i.e., they are not federal district court judges). Decisions of Administrative Law Judges can be appealed to the five-member Board in Washington, D.C.

American Arbitration Association (AAA)—National organization of arbitrators from whose panel arbitrators are selected for labor and civil disputes.

Antitrust Laws—Statutes designed to promote free competition in the market place.

Arbitration—The reference of a dispute to an impartial person chosen by the parties to the dispute who agree in advance to abide by the arbitrator's award issued after a hearing at which both parties have an opportunity to be heard.

Arbitration Acts—Federal and state laws which provide for submission of disputes to the process of arbitration.

Arbitration Board—A panel of arbitrators appointed to hear and decide a dispute according to the rules of arbitration.

Arbitration Clause—A clause inserted in a contract providing for compulsory arbitration in case of a dispute as to the rights or liabilities under such contract.

Arbitrator—A private, disinterested person, chosen by the parties to a disputed question, for the purpose of hearing their contention, and awarding judgment to the prevailing party.

Blue-Collar Workers—Generally refers to individuals engaged in manual labor.

Boycott—A means of exerting pressure on a particular business by refusing to buy its goods or services.

Breach of Contract—The failure, without any legal excuse, to perform any promise which forms the whole or the part of a contract.

Bureau of Labor Statistics—A division of the U.S. Department of Labor that complies statistics related to employment.

Cease and Desist Order—A court order prohibiting an unlawful course of conduct or activity.

Certification—A determination by the NLRB that a particular union is the choice of the majority of the employees.

Charge—An allegation made by an individual, employer or labor organization of an unfair labor practice under the Act. Charges are filed at NLRB's regional offices.

Child Labor Laws—Network of laws on both federal and state levels, prescribing working conditions for children in terms of hours and nature of work which may be performed, all designed to protect the child.

Clayton Act—A federal statute amending the Sherman Antitrust Act.

Closed Shop—A condition contained in the agreement between labor and management that all employees must belong to the union before being hired.

Collective Bargaining—In labor law, refers to the negotiation between employers and employees conducted by a union representative designated by a majority of the employees.

Collective Bargaining Agreement—An Agreement between an employer and a labor union which regulates terms and conditions of employment.

Complaint—If, after investigating a charge, the regional office finds merit and no settlement is reached, the Regional Director serves a complaint in the name of the Board stating the unfair labor practices and containing a notice of hearing before an Administrative Law Judge. The complaint does not constitute a finding of wrongdoing but raises issues to be decided by the judge.

Contract—A contract is an agreement between two or more persons which creates an obligation to do or not to do a particular thing.

Craft Union—A union that limits its members to those who work in a specific craft.

Decertification—The NLRB's withdrawal of a union's authority based on a majority vote of the employees.

Demand for Arbitration—A unilateral filing of a claim in arbitration based on the filer's contractual or statutory right to do so.

Economic Strike—A work stoppage related to a dispute between labor and management over wages, hours or other terms of employment.

Featherbedding—An unfair labor practice whereby the time spent, or number of employees needed, to complete a particular task, is increased unnecessarily for the purpose of creating employment.

Good Faith Bargaining—A mutual obligation placed upon a union and an employer to meet at reasonable times and confer in good faith with respect to wages, hours, and other terms and conditions of employment, or any other matter during the course of the collective bargaining process.

Graft—The fraudulent receipt of public money by a public official.

Grievance—An allegation that there has been a misapplication of some term of a collective bargaining agreement.

Hot Cargo—Contract provision permitting workers to refuse to work on or handle unfair goods coming from a business where a labor dispute is in effect.

Impasse—A deadlock in negotiating between management and officials over terms and conditions of employment.

Independent Contractor—An individual who contracts to perform services for others without qualifying legally as an employee.

Injunction—A judicial remedy either requiring a party to perform an act, or restricting a party from continuing a particular act.

Labor Organization—An association of workers for the purpose of bargaining the terms and conditions of employment on behalf of labor and management.

Labor Dispute—A conflict between a union and an employer.

Labor Law—Legislation dealing with human beings in their capacity as workers or wage earners.

Laissez-Faire—French for "leave alone," refers to the doctrine that an economic system functions best when there is no interference by government. It is based on the belief that the natural economic order tends, when undisturbed by artificial stimulus or regulation, to secure the maximum well-being for the individual and therefore for the community as a whole.

Layoff—A forced furlough from employment, on a temporary basis, generally caused by a lack of available work.

Lockout—A suspension of work initiated by the employer in response to a labor dispute.

Mediation—The act of a third person in intermediating between two contending parties with a view to persuading them to adjust or settle their dispute but without the authority to make a binding decision.

Mediation and Conciliation Service—An independent department of the federal government charged with trying to settle labor disputes by conciliation and mediation.

Mediation/Arbitration—Combination of mediation and arbitration which utilizes a neutral selected to serve as both mediator and arbitrator in a dispute.

Mediator—One who interposes between parties at variance for the purpose of reconciling them.

National Labor Relations Act—A federal statute known as the Wagner Act of 1935 and amended by the Taft-Hartley Act of 1947, which established the National Labor Relations Board to regulate the relations between employers and employees.

National Labor Relations Board—An independent agency created by the National Labor Relations Act of 1935 (Wagner Act), as amended by the acts of 1947 (Taft-Hartley Act) and 1959 (Landrum-Griffin Act), established to regulate the relations between employers and employees.

National Mediation Board—Organization created by Congress in 1934, amending the Railway Labor Act, for the purpose of mediating disputes over wages, hours and working conditions which arise between rail and air carriers, and their employees.

Open Shop—A business in which there is no union or where union membership is not a condition of employment.

Picketing—The announcement of the existence of a labor dispute between labor and management carried out by the employees who generally parade before or near the business with signs publicizing the nature of the dispute.

Quid Pro Quo—Latin for "something for something." Refers to the exchange of promises or performances between two parties. Also refers to the legal consideration necessary to create a binding contract.

Reinstatement—Refers to the return of an employee to employment from which he or she was illegally dismissed.

Scope of Employment—Those activities performed while carrying out the business of one's employer.

Sherman Antitrust Act—A federal statute passed in 1890 to prohibit monopolization and unreasonable restraint of trade in interstate and foreign commerce.

Strike—A concerted stoppage of work by employees.

Sweat Shop—A business which employs workers under poor working conditions at extremely low wages.

Taft-Hartley Act—Refers to the Labor-Management Relations Act of 1947, which was established to prescribe the legitimate rights of both employees and employers.

Temporary Employee—An employee who is hired to work on a short-term basis.

Termination—Refers to cessation of employment, e.g. by quitting or dismissal.

Unconscionable—Refers to a bargain so one-sided as to amount to an absence of meaningful choice on the part of one of the parties, together with terms which are unreasonably favorable to the other party.

Undue Influence—The exertion of improper influence upon another for the purpose of destroying that person's free will in carrying out a particular act, such as entering into a contract.

Unfair Labor Practice—Any activities carried out by either a union or an employer which violate the National Labor Relations Act.

Union Shop—A workplace where all of the employees are members of a union.

Voluntary Arbitration—Arbitration which occurs by mutual and free consent of the parties.

Wildcat Strike—An unauthorized strike for which the union representing the workers disclaims responsibility.

Wrongful Discharge—An unlawful dismissal of an employee.

Zone of Employment—The physical area in which injuries to an employee are covered by worker compensation laws.

BIBLIOGRAPHY AND ADDITIONAL READING

Black's Law Dictionary, Fifth Edition. St. Paul, MN: West Publishing Company, 1979.

Carrell, Michael and Heavrin, Christina *Labor Relations and Collective Bargaining: Cases, Practice, and Law*. New York, NY: Prentice Hall, 1997.

Goldman, Alvin L. *Labor and Employment Law in the United States*. Cambridge, MA: Kluwer Law International, 1996.

Raza, Ali and Anderson, Janelle *Labor Relations and the Law*. New York, NY: Prentice Hall, 1996.

Leader, Sheldon *Freedom of Association: A Study in Labor Law and Political Theory*. New Haven, CT: Yale University Press, 1992

Weiler, Paul C. *Governing the Workplace: The Future of Labor and Employment Law*. Boston, MA: Harvard University Press, 1990.

The National Labor Relations Board (Date Visited: February 2002) <http://www.nlrb.gov/>.

The Society for Human Resources Management (Date Visited: February 2002) <http://www.shrm.org/>.

The United States Department of Labor (Date Visited: February 2002) <http://www.dol.gov/>.

The United States Equal Opportunity Commission (Date Visited: February 2002) <http://www.eeoc.gov/>.

The United States Office of Personnel Management (Date Visited: February 2002) <http://www.opm.gov/>.